PARIS
TO
BOULOGNE

Titles in the Footpaths of Europe Series

Normandy and the Seine
Walking through Brittany
Walks in Provence
Coastal Walks: Normandy and Brittany
Walking the Pyrenees
Walks in the Auvergne
Walks in the Dordogne
Walks in the Loire Valley
Walking the GR5: Modane to Larche
Walking the GR5: Lake Geneva to Mont-Blanc
Paris to Boulogne
Walks in Corsica

The publishers thank the Comité Départemental de Tourisme du
Pas-de-Calais for permission to use their photographs in this book.

PARIS
TO
BOULOGNE

Translated by Danny Price
in association with First Edition

Robertson McCarta

The publishers thank the following people for their help with this book: Isabelle Daguin, Philippe Lambert, Serge Sineux, Daphne Terry

First published in 1990 by

Robertson McCarta Limited
122 King's Cross Road,
London WC1X 9DS

in association with

Fédération Française de Randonnée Pédestre
8 Avenue Marceau
75008 Paris

© Robertson McCarta Limited
© Fédération Française de Randonnée Pédestre
© Maps, Institut Geographique National (French Official Survey)
  and Robertson McCarta Limited.

Managing Editor Folly Marland
Series designed by Prue Bucknall
Production by Grahame Griffiths
Typeset by Columns Limited, Reading
Planning Map by Rodney Paull

Printed and bound in Spain by Graficas Estella S.A.

British Library Cataloguing in Publication Data

Paris to Boulogne — (Footpaths of Europe)
  1. Northern France – Visitors' guides
  I. Series
  914.4'204838

  ISBN 1–85365–114–1

CONTENTS

IGN map legend   6
A note from the publisher   7
Key   8
The footpaths of France, introduction by Robin Neillands   9
Paris to Boulogne, introduction   15

The walks and maps

Walk 1   19

GR124 Cires-les-Mello ▶ Ailly-sur-Noye ▶
Corbie ▶ Rebreuviette

Walk 2   45

GR121 Rebreuviette ▶ Frévent ▶ Hesdin ▶ Montreuil ▶
Boulogne-sur-mer
Tour du Ternois
GR121A Boubers-sur-Canche ▶ Saint-Pol-sur-Ternoise ▶
Anvin ▶ Grigny

Walk 3   75

GR123 Carlepont ▶ Ailly-sur-Noye ▶ Picquigny ▶
Long ▶ Saint-Ricquier ▶ Crécy-en-Ponthieu ▶ Aubin-Saint-Vaast ▶
Hesdin

Walk 4   113

GR127 Arras/Louez-les-Duisans ▶ Maroeuil ▶ Olhain ▶
Pennes-en-Artois ▶ Matringhem ▶ Dennebroeucq
GR127A Dennebroeucq ▶ Verchocq ▶ Hucqueliers ▶ Samer
GR127B Dennebroeucq ▶ Fauquembergues ▶ Merck-Saint-Liévin ▶
Brunembert
Link path GR127 Bours ▶ GR121A Saint-Pol-sur-Ternoise
Le Circuit des Collines de Gohelle
GR127 Bois l'Abbé ▶ Souchez ▶ Liévin ▶ Souches ▶
Ablain-Saint-Nazaire

Walk 5   163

Tour du Boulonnais
GR120 Wissant ▶ Peuplingues ▶ Desvres ▶ Questrecques ▶
Wacquinghen ▶ Cap Gris-Nez ▶ Wissant

Accommodation guide   185
Index   188

Key to IGN Maps

Motorway, dual carriageway _____

Major road, four lanes or more _____

Main road, two-lane or three-lane, wide _____

Main road, two-lane, narrow _____

Narrow road, regularly surfaced _____

Other narrow road: regularly surfaced; irregularly surfaced _____

Possibly private or controlled access

Field track, forest track, felling track, footpath _____

Track of disused road. Road under construction _____

Road through embankment, cutting. Tree-lined road or track _____

Bank. Hedge, line of trees _____

Railway: double track, single track. Electrified line. Station, waiting line. Halt, stop ___

Sidings or access lines. Narrow gauge line. Rack railway _____

Electricity transmission line. Cable railway. Ski lift _____

National boundary with markers _____

Boundary and administrative centre of department, district _____

Boundary and administrative centre of canton, commune _____

For shooting times, go to town hall or gendarmerie

Boundary of military camp, firing range _____

Boundary of State forest, National Park, outer zone of National Park _____

Triangulation points _____

Church, chapel, shrine. Cross, tomb, religious statue. Cemetery _____

Watch tower, fortress. Windmill, wind-pump. Chimney _____

Storage tank: oil, gas. Blast furnace. Pylon. Quarry _____

Cave. Monument, pillar. Castle. Ruins _____

Megalithic monument: dolmen, menhir. Viewpoint. Campsite _____

Market-hall, shed, glasshouse, casemate _____

Access to underground workings. Refuge. Ski-jump _____

Population/thousands _____

183,2   0,4   0,15   0,06

Bridge. Footbridge. Ford. Ferry _____

Lake, pool. Area liable to flooding. Marsh _____

Source, spring. Well, water-tank. Water-tower, reservoir _____

Watercourse lined with trees. Waterfall. Dam. Dyke _____

Navigable canal, feeder or irrigator. Lock, machine-operated. Underground channel:

Contour lines: 10 m. interval. Hollow. Small basin. Scree _____

Principal

Secondary

PF   SP   CT   C

Tr   Chem.   Mon.   P.V.   Mine   Cave   Ch. d'Eau

Woodland   Scrub   Orchard, plantation   Vines   Ricefield

All maps are IGN Orange series. 1:50 000

© I.G.N. – Paris

A note from the publisher

The books in this French Walking Guide series are published in association and with the help of the Fédération Française de la Randonnée Pédestre (French ramblers' association) — generally known as the FFRP.

The FFRP is a federal organisation and is made up of regional, local and many other associations and bodies that form its constituent parts. Individual membership is through these various local organisations. The FFRP therefore acts as an umbrella organisation overseeing the waymarking of footpaths, training and the publishing of the Topoguides, detailed guides to the Grande Randonnée footpaths.

There are at present about 170 Topoguides in print, compiled and written by local members of the FFRP, who are responsible for waymarking the walks — so they are well researched and accurate.

We have translated the main itinerary descriptions, amalgamating and adapting several Topoguides to create new regional guides. We have retained the basic Topoguide structure, indicating length and times of walks, and the Institut Géographique National (official French survey) maps overlaid with the routes.

The information contained in this guide is the latest available at the time of going to print. However, as publishers we are aware that this kind of information is continually changing and we are anxious to enhance and improve the guides as much as possible. We encourage you to send us suggestions, criticisms and those little bits of information you may wish to share with your fellow walkers. Our address is: Robertson-McCarta, 122 King's Cross Road, London WC1X 9DS.

We shall be happy to offer a free copy of any one of these books to any reader whose suggestions are subsequently incorporated into a new edition.

It is possible to create a variety of routes by referring to the walks in the Contents page and to the planning map (inside the front cover). Transport is listed in the alphabetical index in the back of the book and there is an accommodation guide.

KEY

Gournay

This example shows that it is 7km from Gournay to Arbois, and that you can expect it to take 2 hours, 10 minutes.

7Km
2:10

ARBOIS

14th century church

Arbois has a variety of facilities, including hotels and buses. Hotel addresses and bus/train connections may be listed in the index at the back of the book.

a grey arrow indicates an alternative route that leaves and returns to the main route.

Detour

indicates a short detour off the route to a town with facilities or to an interesting sight.

Symbols:

hotel;
youth hostel, hut or refuge;
camping;
restaurant;
cafe;·

shops;
railway station;
buses;
ferry;
tourist information.

THE FOOTPATHS OF FRANCE

by Robin Neillands

Why should you go walking in France? Well, walking is fun and as for France, Danton summed up the attractions of that country with one telling phrase: 'Every man has two countries,' he said, 'his own . . . and France.' That is certainly true in my case and I therefore consider it both a pleasure and an honour to write this general introduction to these footpath guides to France. A pleasure because walking in or through France is my favourite pastime, an honour because these excellent English language guides follow in the course set by those Topo-guides published in French by the Fédération Française pour la Randonnée Pédestre, which set a benchmark for quality that all footpath guides might follow. Besides, I believe that good things should be shared and walking in France is one of the most pleasant activities I know.

I have been walking in France for over thirty years. I began by rambling — or rather ambling — through the foothills of the Pyrenees, crossing over into Spain past the old Hospice de France, coming back over the Somport Pass in a howling blizzard, which may account for the fact that I totally missed two sets of frontier guards on both occasions. Since then I have walked in many parts of France and even from one end of it to the other, from the Channel to the Camargue, and I hope to go on walking there for many years to come.

The attractions of France are legion, but there is no finer way to see and enjoy them than on foot. France has two coasts, at least three mountain ranges — the Alps, Pyrenees and the Massif Central — an agreeable climate, a great sense of space, good food, fine wines and, believe it or not, a friendly and hospitable people. If you don't believe me, go there on foot and see for yourself. Walking in France will appeal to every kind of walker, from the day rambler to the backpacker, because above all, and in the nicest possible way, the walking in France is well organised, but those Francophiles who already know France well, will find it even more pleasureable if they explore their favourite country on foot.

The GR system

The Grande Randonnée (GR) footpath network now consists of more than 40,000 kilometres (25,000 miles) of long-distance footpath, stretching into every part of France, forming a great sweep around Paris, probing deeply into the Alps, the Pyrenees, and the volcanic cones of the Massif Central. This network, the finest system of footpaths in Europe, is the creation of that marvellously named organisation, *la Fédération Française de Randonnée Pédestre, Comité National des Sentiers de Grande Randonnée*, which I shall abbreviate to FFRP-CNSGR. Founded in 1948, and declaring that, *'un jour de marche, huit jours de santé,'* the FFRP-CNSGR has flourished for four decades and put up the now familiar red-and-white waymarks in every corner of the country. Some of these footpaths are classic walks, like the famous GR65, *Le Chemin de St Jacques*, the ancient Pilgrim Road to Compostela, the TMB, the *Tour du Mont Blanc*, which circles the mountain through France, Switzerland and Italy, or the 600-mile long GR3, the *Sentier de la Loire*, which runs from the Ardèche to the Atlantic, to give three examples from the hundred or so GR trails available. In addition there is an abundance of GR du Pays or regional footpaths, like the *Sentier de la Haute Auvergne*, and the *Sentier Tour des Monts d'Aubrac*. A 'Tour' incidentally, is usually a circular walk. Many of these regional or provincial GR trails are charted and waymarked in red-and-yellow by local outdoor organisations such as ABRI (Association Bretonne des Relais et Itineraires) for Brittany, or CHAMINA for the Massif Central. The walker in France will soon become familiar with all these footpath networks, national, regional or local, and find them the perfect way into the heart and heartland of France. As a little bonus, the GR networks are expanding all the time, with the detours — or *varientes* — off the main route eventually linking with other GR paths or *varientes* and becoming GR trails in their own right.

Walkers will find the GR trails generally well marked and easy to follow, and they have two advantages over the footpaths commonly encountered in the UK. First, since they are laid out by local people, they are based on intricate local knowledge of the local sights. If there is a fine view, a mighty castle or a pretty village on your footpath route, your footpath through France will surely lead you to it. Secondly, all French footpaths are usually well provided with a wide range of comfortable country accommodation, and you will discover that the local people, even the farmers, are well used to walkers and greet them with a smile, a '*Bonjour*' and a '*bon route*'.

Terrain and climate
As a glance at these guides or any Topo-guide will indicate, France has a great variety of terrain. France is twice the size of the UK and many natural features are also on a larger scale. There are three main ranges of mountains: the Alps contain the highest mountain in Europe, the Pyrenees go up to 10,000 ft, the Massif Central peaks to over 6000 ft, and there are many similar ranges with hills which overtop our highest British peak, Ben Nevis. On the other hand, the Auvergne and the Jura have marvellous open ridge walking, the Cévennes are steep and rugged, the Ardèche and parts of Provence are hot and wild, the Île de France, Normandy, Brittany and much of Western France is green and pleasant, not given to extremes. There is walking in France for every kind of walker, but given such a choice the wise walker will consider the complications of terrain and weather before setting out, and go suitably equipped.

France enjoys three types of climate: continental, oceanic and mediterranean. South of the Loire it will certainly be hot to very hot from mid-April to late September. Snow can fall on the mountains above 4,000 ft from mid-October and last until May, or even lie year-round on the tops and in couloirs; in the high hills an ice-axe is never a frill. I have used one by the Brêche de Roland in the Pyrenees in mid-June.

Wise walkers should study weather maps and forecasts carefully in the week before they leave for France, but can generally expect good weather from May to October, and a wide variety of weather — the severity depending on the terrain — from mid-October to the late Spring.

Accommodation
The walker in France can choose from a wide variety of accommodation with the assurance that the walker will always be welcome. This can range from country hotels to wild mountain pitches, but to stay in comfort, many walkers will travel light and overnight in the comfortable hotels of the *Logis de France* network.

Logis de France: The *Logis de France* is a nationwide network of small, family-run country hotels, offering comfortable accommodation and excellent food. *Logis* hotels are graded and can vary from a simple, one-star establishment, with showers and linoleum, to a four- or five-star *logis* with gastronomic menus and deep-pile carpets. All offer excellent value for money, and since there are over 5,000 scattered across the

French countryside, they provide a good focus for a walking day. An annual guide to the *Logis* is available from the French Government Tourist Office, 178 Piccadilly, London W1V 0AL, Tel. (01) 491 7622.

Gîtes d'étape: A *gîte d'étape* is best imagined as an unmanned youth hostel for outdoor folk of all ages. They lie all along the footpath networks and are usually signposted or listed in the guides. They can be very comfortable, with bunk beds, showers, a well equipped kitchen, and in some cases they have a warden, a *guardien*, who may offer meals. *Gîtes d'étape* are designed exclusively for walkers, climbers, cyclists, cross country skiers or horse-riders. A typical price (1990) would be Fr.25 for one night. *Gîtes d'étape* should not be confused with a *Gîte de France*. A *gîte* — usually signposted as '*Gîte de France*' — is a country cottage available for a holiday let, though here too, the owner may be more than willing to rent it out as overnight accommodation.

Youth hostels: Curiously enough, there are very few Youth Hostels in France outside the main towns. A full list of the 200 or so available can be obtained from the Youth Hostel Association (YHA), Trevelyan House, St Albans, Herts AL1 2DY.

Pensions or cafes: In the absence of an hotel, a *gîte d'étape* or a youth hostel, all is not lost. France has plenty of accommodation and an enquiry at the village cafe or bar will usually produce a room. The cafe/hotel may have rooms or suggest a nearby pension or a *chambre d'hôte*. Prices start at around Fr.50 for a room, rising to, say, Fr.120. (1990 estimate).

Chambres d'hôte: A *chambre d'hôte* is a guest room or, in English terms, a bed-and-breakfast, usually in a private house. Prices range up from about Fr.60 a night. *Chambres d'hôte* signs are now proliferating in the small villages of France and especially if you can speak a little French are an excellent way to meet the local people. Prices (1990) are from, say, Fr.70 a night for a room, not per person.

Abris: *Abris*, shelters or mountain huts can be found in the mountain regions, where they are often run by the *Club Alpin Français*, an association for climbers. They range from the comfortable to the primitive, are often crowded and are sometimes reserved for members. Details from the Club Alpin Français, 7 Rue la Boétie, Paris 75008, France.

Camping: French camp sites are graded from one to five star, but are generally very good at every level, although the facilities naturally vary from one cold tap to shops, bars and heated pools. Walkers should not be deterred by a '*Complet*' (Full) sign on the gate or office window: a walker's small tent will usually fit in somewhere. *Camping à la ferme*, or farm camping, is increasingly popular, more primitive — or less regimented — than the official sites, but widely available and perfectly adequate. Wild camping is officially not permitted in National Parks, but unofficially if you are over 1,500m away from a road, one hour's walk from a *gîte* or campsite, and where possible ask permission, you should have no trouble. French country people will always assist the walker to find a pitch.

The law for walkers
The country people of France seem a good deal less concerned about their 'rights'

than the average English farmer or landowner. I have never been ordered off land in France or greeted with anything other than friendliness . . . maybe I've been lucky. As a rule, walkers in France are free to roam over all open paths and tracks. No decent walker will leave gates open, trample crops or break down walls, and taking fruit from gardens or orchards is simply stealing. In some parts of France there are local laws about taking chestnuts, mushrooms (and snails), because these are cash crops. Signs like *Réserve de Chasse*, or *Chasse Privé* indicate that the shooting is reserved for the landowner. As a general rule, behave sensibly and you will be tolerated everywhere, even on private land.

The country code

Walkers in France should obey the *Code du Randonneur*:

- Love and respect Nature.
- Avoid unnecessary noise.
- Destroy nothing.
- Do not leave litter.
- Do not pick flowers or plants.
- Do not disturb wildlife.
- Re-close all gates.
- Protect and preserve the habitat.
- No smoking or fires in the forests. (This rule is essential and is actively enforced by foresters and police.)
- Stay on the footpath.
- Respect and understand the country way of life and the country people.
- Think of others as you think of yourself.

Transport

Transportation to and within France is generally excellent. There are no less than nine Channel ports: Dunkirk, Calais, Boulogne, Dieppe, Le Havre, Caen/Ouistreham, Cherbourg, Saint-Malo and Roscoff, and a surprising number of airports served by direct flights from the UK. Although some of the services are seasonal, it is often possible to fly direct to Toulouse, Poitiers, Nantes, Perpignan, Montpellier, indeed to many provincial cities, as well as to Paris and such obvious destinations as Lyon and Nice. Within France the national railway, the SNCF, still retains a nationwide network. Information, tickets and a map can be obtained from the SNCF. France also has a good country bus service and the *gare routière* is often placed just beside the railway station. Be aware though, that many French bus services only operate within the *département*, and they do not generally operate from one provincial city to the next. I cannot encourage people to hitch-hike, which is both illegal and risky, but walkers might consider a taxi for their luggage. Almost every French village has a taxi driver who will happily transport your rucksacks to the next night-stop, fifteen to twenty miles away, for Fr.50 a head or even less.

Money

Walking in France is cheap, but banks are not common in the smaller villages, so carry a certain amount of French money and the rest in traveller's cheques or Eurocheques, which are accepted everywhere.

Clothing and equipment

The amount of clothing and equipment you will need depends on the terrain, the length of the walk, the time of your visit, the accommodation used. Outside the mountain areas it is not necessary to take the full range of camping or backpacking gear. I once walked across France from the Channel to the Camargue along the Grande Randonnée footpaths in March, April and early May and never needed to use any of the camping gear I carried in my rucksack because I found hotels everywhere, even in quite small villages.

Essential items are:

In summer: light boots, a hat, shorts, suncream, lip salve, mosquito repellent, sunglasses, a sweater, a windproof cagoule, a small first-aid kit, a walking stick.
In winter: a change of clothing, stormproof outer garments, gaiters, hat, lip salve, a companion.
In the mountains at any time: large-scale maps (1:25,000), a compass, an ice-axe. In winter, add a companion and ten-point crampons.
At any time: a phrase book, suitable maps, a dictionary, a sense of humour.

The best guide to what to take lies in the likely weather and the terrain. France tends to be informal, so there is no need to carry a jacket or something smart for the evenings. I swear by Rohan clothing, which is light, smart and functional. The three things I would never go without are light, well-broken-in boots and several pairs of loop-stitched socks, and my walking stick.

Health hazards

Health hazards are few. France can be hot in summer, so take a full water-bottle and refill it at every opportunity. A small first-aid kit is sensible, with plasters and 'mole-skin' for blisters, but since prevention is better than cure, loop-stitched socks and flexible boots are better. Any French chemist — a *pharmacie* — is obliged to render first-aid treatment for a small fee. These pharmacies can be found in most villages and large towns and are marked by a green cross.

Dogs are both a nuisance and a hazard. All walkers in France should carry a walking stick to fend off aggressive curs. Rabies — *la rage* — is endemic and anyone bitten must seek immediate medical advice. France also possesses two types of viper, which are common in the hill areas of the south. In fairness, although I found my walking stick indispensable, I must add that in thirty years I have never even seen a snake or a rabid dog. In case of real difficulty, dial 17 for the police and the ambulance.

Food and wine

One of the great advantages with walking in France is that you can end the day with a good meal and not gain an ounce. French country cooking is generally excellent and good value for money, with the price of a four-course menu starting at about Fr.45. The ingredients for the mid-day picnic can be purchased from the village shops and these also sell wine. Camping-Gaz cylinders and cartridges are widely available, as is 2-star petrol for stoves. Avoid naked fires.

Preparation

The secret of a good walk lies in making adequate preparations before you set out. It pays to be fit enough to do the daily distance at the start. Much of the necessary information is contained in this guide, but if you need more, look in guidebooks or outdoor magazines, or ask friends.

The French

I cannot close this introduction without saying a few words about the French, not least because the walker in France is going to meet rather more French people than, say, a motorist will, and may even meet French people who have never met a foreigner before. It does help if the visitor speaks a little French, even if only enough to say '*bonjour*' and '*Merci*' and '*S'il vous plaît*'. The French tend to be formal and it pays to be polite, to say 'hello', to shake hands. I am well aware that relations between France and England have not always been cordial over the last six hundred years or so, but I have never met with hostility of any kind in thirty years of walking through France. Indeed, I have always found that if the visitor is prepared to meet the French halfway, they will come more than halfway to greet him or her in return, and are both friendly and hospitable to the passing stranger.

As a final tip, try smiling. Even in France, or especially in France, a smile and a '*pouvez vous m'aider?*' (Can you help me?) will work wonders. That's my last bit of advice, and all I need do now is wish you '*Bonne Route*' and good walking in France.

PARIS TO BOULOGNE

The footpaths in Walks 1 and 3 cross Picardy, a region steeped in more than 1,000 years of history and featuring vast sweeps of cultivated plains broken by numerous valleys where picturesque little villages cling to the hillsides and offer some quite breathtaking views. In addition, there are several attractive small towns, such as Picquigny and Corbie, with much of interest to detain the visitor.

The valleys are broad and gently sloping, often marshy, with small lakes and peat bogs, or watered by lazily meandering rivers. On its way from the Ile-de-France to the Boulonnais country, the path takes walkers through the Thérain, Brèche and Somme valleys, all of which are quite different in character. Walkers will also come across the unusual. Just after setting out from Cires-lès-Mello, for example, not far from the path near Saint-Vaast, there is a fascinating area full of quarries. A century ago the fine local limestone was extracted in massive quantities to satisfy the huge demand for building stone generated by Baron Haussman's ambitious building programme for Paris.

The Somme is the largest of Picardy's waterways. The GR123 and GR124 intersect at Ailly-sur-Noye. From here the GR123 runs through the valley of the Somme below Amiens, while the GR124 heads north, towards Corbie. In the valley around Amiens are the *hortillonnages*, market gardens. Situated in marshlands, the produce is transported in curious punt-like boats, indeed the gardens can only be reached by water.

There are several interesting places locally to see as well. Picquigny, for example, from where, on a clear day, views stretch as far as Amiens. A strategically important little town, it was here in 1475 that the warring kings, Louis XI of France and Edward IV of England, finally met to end their disputes. The degree of mutual trust between the two men was such however that in the lodge where they met bars were used to separate them, inspiring the chronicler Commines to write that the lodge reminded him of a lion's cage! Mme. de Sévigné's country house can be visited and the remains of the imposing ramparts built of sandstone blocks seen. Also in this part of the valley is Ailly-sur-Somme whose church has a roof so enormous it is reminiscent of the sail of a boat. Bourdon, Bouchon and Cocquerel have churches which are typical of Picardy, while at Long there is a fine château open to visitors.

After crossing the Somme, the GR123 heads through the region of Ponthieu, famous for the flowers that adorn its villages. Millencourt is one of these, with traditional houses with cob gables; Canchy is another, and Ailly-le-Haut-Clocher, perched on its high hill, is a reminder of the last war when the Germans used it as an observation post.

Picardy has some particularly beautiful forests. Leaving the Thérain valley behind, the path enters the forest of Hez-Froidmont, also known as the forest of Neuville. Isolated from the other woodlands north of Paris, its trees cover 3,000 hectares of dark narrow valleys.

East of Thérain, the GR124A brings us to the Compiègne forest. This route is well known and leads into the southern part of the forest, to the Acaste intersection, quite near the ruins at Champlieu and the Grands Monts, both well worth a visit.

As it nears the end of its journey across Picardy, the GR123 passes through the forest of Crécy. One of the first great battles of the Hundred Years' War, disastrous for the French, the spot where it was fought, Crécy-en-Ponthieu, is situated at the northern edge of the forest. A royal hunting forest, it was a favourite with Louis XI.

The walks in this region also have a spiritual theme. The GR123 passes several abbeys along its route. Nearest to the Ile-de-France is Ourscamps, founded at the beginning of the 12th century by St Bernard. All that remains intact is that part dating from the 18th century, but the ruins are just as romantic as those at Jumièges and it is surrounded by a long and most impressive wall. In the Somme, not far from Picquigny, the abbey of Le Gard blends harmoniously into the landscape. The abbey was Cistercian and Cardinal Mazarin, Louis XIII's chief minister after Richelieu, was once its abbot. Besides the impressive ruins of the original abbey, there is another large abbey building with a fine central pediment. After crossing the Somme in the heart of Ponthieu, the walker will reach Saint-Riquier, named after the monk from Picardy of the same name.

As the GR123 nears the end of its route through Picardy it comes to the River Authie not far from the abbey of Valloires. This Cistercian abbey blends harmoniously with the surrounding countryside. Its stonework is remarkably delicate, but the most striking feature of this elegant and well preserved building is its wood panelling.

The GR121
Running east to west from Bon-Secours in Belgium to Equihen in the Côte d'Opale, the GR121 is the first long-distance footpath to cross the Nord and Pas-de-Calais *départements*. An area often neglected by the tourist, the sometimes solitary, sometimes wild landscapes offer the walker both peace and tranquillity.

In this guide, Walk 2 follows the route of the GR121 from Rebreuviette in the Canche valley, taking you forward on the journey to Boulogne from the point where Walk 1 and the GR124 ended. The Canche valley is famed for the flowers that adorn every village and which can be appreciated from the river bank, the hillsides, or from the path as it twists and turns across the plateau. A sudden change of scenery announces the more rugged and hilly Boulonnais country, beyond which lies the Côte d'Opale with its dunes, vast beaches and bracing climate.

The GR121A, Tour du Ternois
The Ternois is situated between the plain of Picardy to the south, the coastal strip to the west, the high country of the Artois and the Artois hills to the north. To the east is the Artois plateau where the valleys of the Rivers Scarpe and Gy form the only depressions. It forms a geographical entity, just 2 hours from the large regional centre of Lille and 45 minutes from the coal fields, along the route that holidaymakers take on their way to the Côte d'Opale and is itself a favourite holiday centre.

The three valleys of the Rivers Authie, Canche and Ternoise cross the Ternois from south-east to north-west, but there are many other valleys feeding into them, most of them riverless. Only the valleys and the areas immediately surrounding the villages are really green. In the wet valley bottoms, marshes provide a sanctuary for animals and birds and form wide expanses of natural countryside. The uniformity of the rolling plateaux, given over to large-scale farming, contrasts with the variety of the valley landscapes with their fields criss-crossed by hedgerows. The richness of the Ternois landscape is completed by large areas of woodland. The land varies from a height of 40 metres above sea level, at Wail, to 170 metres, at Grand-Rullencourt. In many places there are gorges and cliffs where the ever-present limestone is exposed. As you walk the Ternois footpath, you will not only get back to nature, but also discover something of the way of life of the friendly people who live and work there.

This 54 kilometre footpath is linked to the GR121, providing an alternative to it over this distance. If you carry on along the 18 kilometres of the GR121, you can do a circular 72 kilometre tour which will take you between two and three days to complete.

The Ternois footpath is also linked to the GR127 by a path 15.7 kilometres long between Saint-Pol-sur-Ternoise and Bours, which makes it possible to complete a circular tour taking three or four days, using both the GR121 and GR127.

The GR127: the Artois hills

This long-distance footpath follows the Artois hills and links the Arras region with Artois and the Boulogne area. The hills form an escarpment along the fault line between two geological and geographical regions, the Paris Basin and the Flanders Plain. The very attractive pastoral walk varies in height and landscape; leaving the Scarpe valley, it crosses the river valleys of the Lys and the Aa, past the sources of the rivers Course and Liane, and through woods and picturesque villages with fine châteaux and beautiful churches.

The route climbs first past the ruins of the ancient abbey of Mont Saint Eloi, then a view over the Canadian monument at Vimy, to the chapel, watch-tower and military cemetery of Notre Dame de Lorette, all three commemorating action there in the 1914–1918 War. Next it winds along the departmental base of Olhain, with an 18-hole golf-course and mediaeval castle, before reaching the mediaeval fortress of Bours which serves as the village mairie. The Flanders hills are visible from the plateau, and the path continues to Amettes, past the birthplace of the great European traveller Saint Benoit Labre — a modest 18th-century house of typical Artois style.

Going north, Bergneules at 206m — 'the roof of the Pas-de-Calais' — dominates the Boulogne 'bocage', the area of hedges and small fields, and at Quesques the footpath joins the GR120, the Tour du Boulonnais (Tour of the Boulogne region).

Southwards, the path follows the river Aa and then runs close to the river Course. Beyond Doudeauville it joins the GR121, leading on to the route of the coastline GR and the port of Boulogne-sur-Mer.

Tour du Boulonnais

Called the Boulonnais Footpath (because it includes much of the area around Boulogne), the GR120 is some 130 kilometres long. It is part of a network of seven footpaths amounting to some 1,000 kilometres which cross the Nord and Pas-de-Calais *départements*, forming an important addition to the national network of 30,000 kilometres of footpath throughout France.

A circular tour, the GR120 gives a unique insight into the varied scenery of this compact region, far more picturesque than many of the descriptions of northern France would lead us to believe.

Seascape alternates with open countryside, pasture with forest. It starts near the vast expanse of fine sandy beaches at Wissant, crosses three large state forests, winds among fertile plains and grassy slopes, then returns gradually towards the coast.

The undulating landscape provides some splendid views, adding further to the delights of an already interesting footpath (the Mont de Couple is a case in point).

Woods and meadows intermingle, streams dash along stony beds. Hedges, where holly and hawthorn grow alongside willow, line the little pathways. Everywhere you look there are long, low houses, many of them white-fronted, with red roofs and colourful, flower-decked windows. These are houses in the traditional Boulonnais style, though it is true that they are being replaced by modern buildings of a more uniform kind.

From the GR120 it is also possible to branch off along part of the *sentier du littoral* (coastal footpath). Staying close to the coast, the route runs along cliff-tops, skirting their bases, crossing stretches of sand or winding among rocks. In just a few days the walker can get to know the Boulonnais with its delightful blend of land and sea.

Though Boulonnais was undoubtedly inhabited during the Stone Age, the history of the region only really began in Roman times. The largest port in the region was Portus Itius, probably modern-day Boulogne or possible Wissant. From there Caesar started out for England, but it was the Emperor Claudius who succeeded in founding a Roman province in Britain and made Gesoriacum (Boulogne) the home port of the Classis Britannica (British Fleet).

Throughout the Middle Ages Boulonnais was the scene of many conflicts, but by the time of the Revolution Boulogne had become relatively prosperous. The seafarers of Boulogne played their part in the defence of an endangered nation. England became more than ever the traditional enemy, and the buccaneers entered wholeheartedly into the spirit of it, especially as, under Napoleon, Boulogne had regained a military role. The troops of the Grande Armée were massed there. Napoleon himself stayed for a short while at the Château de Pont-de-Briques. Both the Colonne de la Grande Armée and a little monument near the cliff at Terlincthun commemorate the official distribution of the insignia of the Légion d'Honneur by Napoleon.

The 1914–18 war caused relatively little damage compared with that inflicted between 1939 and 1945. Even now traces of the Second World War are to be seen: the whole coastline is studded with blockhouses and the hinterland bears signs of the military installations whose main aims were to frustrate an allied landing in this sector and to launch V1 attacks against England, a mere 40 kilometres away. The concentration of German defences explains the intensity with which the whole coastal area was bombarded, and it is noticeable that in many villages there are virtually no houses much more than forty years old.

Fortunately the history of Boulonnais is not full of memories of war alone. The architectural heritage is no less interesting. There are many old churches, some of which are so discreetly tucked away that the tourist in a hurry misses them. Take for example Pittefaux, Le Wast, or Houllefort; and still others looking for all the world like fortresses: Audresselles, Longueville, Nabringhen and Licques.

It would be unthinkable not to mention the many châteaux which, even if not visited, are sufficiently attractive from the outside to warrant stopping for a second look The Château d'Odre near La Capelle, the Château de Colembert; those of Wierre-au-Bois and Souverain-Moulin (Pittefaux) and the châteaux of the Denacre valley (Wimille). The list could go on. This legacy is part of the attraction of the Boulonnais region and was no doubt appreciated by a number of the great figures who chose to live here, such as the young Sainte-Beauve, Charles Dickens, René Bazin and the painter Gil Franco.

At the present time, natural resources are still at the heart of the region's economy. The rich variety of its geological resources form the basis of its industrial development: cement manufacturing at Desvres and Dannes, famous ceramics at Desvres, where art and industry meet, and marble quarries at Marquise. Even the metal industry has its origins in former deposits of ore.

There is too agriculture, mainly concentrating on animal husbandry in lower Boulonnais, while in the north, around Wissant and Guines, cereals and commercial crops such as sugar-beet, potatoes and chicory are grown.

It is the sea which governs Boulogne's main business activities, however. Boulogne remains the foremost fishing port in the European Community, and the second most important travel port in France after Calais, thanks to its ship and hovercraft services to England.

WALK 1

CIRES-LÈS-MELLO
🏠 ✕ 🍷 ⚒

(see map ref 21)
13th century tithe barn. In
the church, 12th century
historiated capitals and 15th
and 16th century statues.

10Km
2:30

MÉRARD
🍷 ⚒

As you leave the railway station, go over the level crossing and carry straight on down the Rue de la Ville until you come to the D929. Turn right here and then take the first on the left (road to Foulangues).

As you climb you will see the GR124 waymark just before you get to the cemetery. Take the path which climbs to the right. At the intersection 800 metres further on take the sunken path down to the right running alongside a wall. Then take a path to the left which climbs steeply and overlooks the village. Further on, it crosses the D929. Take the path opposite going down to the left through a small wood. Cross the railway line and then the River Thérain. About 500 metres further on you come to Saint-Claude.

The GR turns left along the D12 for 400 metres. At the wayside cross, turn on to a path climbing north-west through undergrowth. When you come to a barn turn right and 1 kilometre further on (spot height 102) head left. As it comes to a small pine wood the GR twice turns sharply to the right, then skirts the Vallée Gauthier. Cross the D137 and take the path almost opposite. About 100 metres further on take the path to the right and follow it for 1·2 kilometres until you come to a tarred path. Turn left and, just after passing the water tower, turn right. The road here runs alongside a small wood, bears left and comes out between two fields. In the second wood, take the right-hand path running alongside an old quarry, which is fenced off. When you come to the gate into the quarry, turn left on to a path which is scarcely visible to begin with. Follow this down through the wood and you come to Mérard.

The GR124 goes through the village and reaches the D144E. Turn left on to this and then take the road on the right just after the cemetery. About 100 metres further on take the path which climbs to the right. The GR

4Km
1:10

Ansacq
Old manor, fortified by
Cardinal Mazarin.
Junction with the GR225.

2Km
0:45

THURY-SOUS-CLERMONT
(see map ref 22)

7Km
1:45

Fay-sous-Bois
(see map ref 23)
Here the GR124 and the
GR225 split.

1Km
0:20

Le Mont de Hermes
(see map ref 24)
Detour *45 minutes*
HERMES
The route is marked by a
broken line on the map.

2Km
0:30

climbs through pines, reaches the crest, then runs alongside an old quarry overgrown by trees. Continue in the same direction for 1·5 kilometres. After passing under the power line the GR drops down, veers sharply right and joins up with the D144E at Vieux Château farm. Turn left along the road to reach Ansacq.

At the T junction (spot height 71) turn left. At the wayside cross take the path opposite climbing up through the wood. When you come out of the wood take the path to the left. Cross the D929. The GR drops down through a wood, crosses some pasture and joins up with a path. Follow this path to the left until you reach a road. Turn right, cross a street and you come to Thury-sous-Clermont.

Turn left along the D89 and 50 metres further on turn right into a road skirting a housing estate. At the top of the hill turn left on to a path which passes a reservoir and then drops down to the D55, which you cross. Take the road leading down into Fillerval. Pass near the château and as you leave the hamlet, take the path to the right to enter the Forêt de Hez-Froidmont. Follow the path through the forest until you come to Poteau de la Verrière, where you turn left. At the next intersection take the path opposite that climbs, leaving a forest track on the right. At the next fork take the path to the right. As you come out of the forest, follow a path to the left running beside a field. Continue until you come to Fay-sous-Bois, where you take the path to the right and a little later (spot height 79) turn left until you get to the western edge of Fay-sous-Bois.

At this point the GR124 turns right and goes up Val Hermont. When you reach the top you come to a place known as Le Mont de Hermes.

From Mont de Hermes the GR124 continues straight on, crosses a field and goes into the forest to reach the forest road near the Maison Forestière de Froidmont (forester's house).

21

Maison Forestière de Froidmont

Nearby are the ruins of the 12th century abbey, L'Abbaye de Froidmont.

7Km
1:45

In front of the forester's house take the right-hand path, passing above a spring, the Fontaine Chaudron, and continuing until you come to a place where four paths meet. Take the middle one. Further on, at a place known as Le Gravier, take the path that climbs to the left. Pass to the west of the Croix Grand-Jean intersection, cross two other paths and continue down to the D55. Turn left onto this and continue until you come to La Neuville-en-Hez.

LA NEUVILLE-EN-HEZ

(see map ref 25)
Church with 12th century tower and 15th century chancel.

3Km
0:45

Go along the road until you come to the N31. Cross over and almost opposite take the first street on the left. Just before you get to the church turn right. Go between the cemetery and the sports ground and again enter the forest. Later you come to an intersection of six paths. Carry straight on, crossing the track of a disused railway. At a clearing (spot height 75) turn left and leave the wood to arrive at the junction with the GR124A.

Junction with the GR124A.

(see map ref 26)

2Km
0:30

The GR124 turns left to run alongside a copse, the Bosquet Lipus. Cross the D55 and follow the D537 opposite to reach Litz.

LITZ

6.5Km
1:40

Go through the village and take the right-hand road passing in front of the church. At the water tower, head left and take a road on the right which runs alongside a disused railway line to come to Wariville. As you come out of the hamlet turn right. Further on turn into a wood, the Bois du Houssoy. When you come to the intersection with the D94 turn right to reach Bulles.

BULLES

8Km
2:00

After passing the church, turn right onto the D151 and before you reach the track of the old railway line take a path to the left. A little further on you pick up the track of the old railway, which you follow for 4 kilometres. Turn left onto the road near an old railway station. Further on take the path going down through the trees. Once more turn right along the road until you reach a wayside cross. Turn right onto the path nearest the cross. At the next fork (spot height 142) take the path on the left. Cross the D94 and you are in Le Mesnil-sur-Bulles.

Le Mesnil-sur-Bulles
(see map ref 27)

6Km
1:30

BUCAMPS

5Km
1:15

MONTREUIL-SUR-BRÊCHE

7Km
1:45

REUIL-SUR-BRÊCHE

(see map ref 28)

11Km
2:45

At the crossroads just before the cemetery (spot height 148) turn right. Further on you cross the D938. Carry on until you get to a farm, the Ferme de Busmaubert. Carry straight on, going north-west, towards a wood, the Bois Ragon, and follow the path along its southern edge. Head towards another wood, the Bois de Bucamps. Again follow the path along its southern edge and meet up with the D61 as you come into Bucamps.

Go through the village and just before you reach the cemetery turn left. At the fork bear left. Further on you cross a road and go down into the valley. Here you cross another road, which you rejoin later. When you reach the wayside cross turn right and at the next crossroads turn left into Montreuil-sur-Brêche.

Head west along the D151. Turn left onto the D125, which crosses the Brêche. When you get to a cross take the path opposite. Further on, as you come to the end of a fence, turn right. Here the GR runs beside a tumulus topped by a cross, known as Croix-de-la-Motte. When you reach the bottom of the hill take the left-hand path which runs along the side of a wood, the Bois du Jardinet, and then turns left. At the next intersection turn right and a little further on left, then right again to cross the area known as Domaine de Mauregard. Bear right at the fork and drop down through a wood. Just before you come to the bridge over the Brêche you arrive at Reuil-sur-Brêche.

Before reaching the bridge the GR takes the left-hand path running along beside the river. Further on turn left, and at the wayside cross turn right to reach the D561. Turn left onto this road. At the fork take the road leading off to the right, then a little further on the path going right towards the water tower. Carry on until you reach a small wood. Follow the path along its eastern, then its northern edge. Take the path to La Fosse-aux-Rieux on the right and cross a road. Pass east of La Neuville-Saint-Pierre and cross the D34. Follow the path opposite as it climbs up through a wood, the Bois de Bas. Turn right and at the intersection near a farm, the Ferme de Moimont, take the

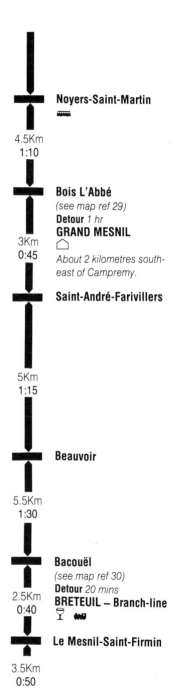

Noyers-Saint-Martin

4.5Km
1:10

Bois L'Abbé
(see map ref 29)
Detour *1 hr*
GRAND MESNIL
△
About 2 kilometres south-east of Campremy.

3Km
0:45

Saint-André-Farivillers

5Km
1:15

Beauvoir

5.5Km
1:30

Bacouël
(see map ref 30)
Detour *20 mins*
BRETEUIL – Branch-line
🍷 🚆

2.5Km
0:40

Le Mesnil-Saint-Firmin

3.5Km
0:50

right-hand path, which passes under a power line and comes to a road. Turn right onto this road. At the wayside cross turn left and cross the D151 just north-west of Noyers-St-Martin.

Continue in the same direction, crossing an old railway line. At the cross take the path to the left. A little further on head towards the right to reach the path above a farm, the Ferme Noirvaux. Here you turn right and go down the path to Bois L'Abbé.

Go through the hamlet of Bois l'Abbé and, at the crossroads after the square, take the road to the left then the path to the left, which runs along the Vallée Jean-Quarry. When you reach the D61 follow it to the left and continue until you come to St-André-Farivillers.

In the village you come to a high bank on the left, where you take the road on the right. A little further on go down a path on the left, which leads to an intersection. Turn right and follow the path up towards a wood, the Bois de Calmont. Turn right at the water tower, and then pick up a road, which you follow to the left. As you come into the hamlet of Evauchaux, turn left and cross the D916 at a place known as La Folie. Carry straight on and at the water tower turn left to come to Beauvoir.

As you walk north out of the village take a road to the right for 750 metres. Follow a path to the right until you reach the old Roman road known as the Chaussée Brunehaut. Turn right and at the next intersection (spot height 114) turn left. The GR carries straight on, crosses the D90 and comes to Bacouël.

At the junction as you come into Bacouël take the right-hand fork. Cross the D117, go under a railway line and you come to Le Mesnil-St-Firmin.

Before reaching the village take the road to the left. Cross the D930 and a little further on follow a path to the right, which heads north-east towards Rocquencourt.

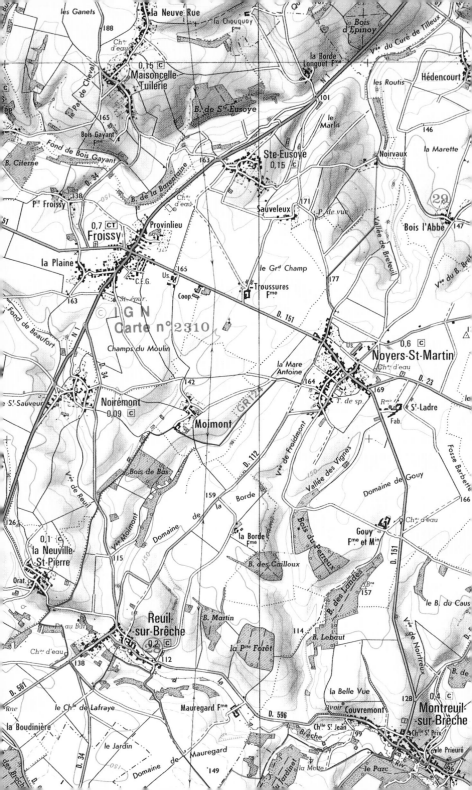

Rocquencourt

6Km
1:30

Follow the main street through the village and at the fork take the road on the left. Follow the footpath along the Vallée des Merles. In the Bois du Câtillon, cross a departmental road and just after this head to the right along a path until you reach the Chapelle St-Vincent to the west of Folleville.

Folleville
Ruins of the 15th century château; church dating from the 15th and 16th centuries. Relic of St Vincent-de-Paul, who crossed the lands of the fief of Folleville in 1617.

4Km
1:00

Cross the D14 and go under the railway bridge. Further on turn left onto the D109 until you reach a shrine near La Faloise.

LA FALOISE
✕ ￼ ⚓ 🚌
(see map ref 31)
Château dating from the 15th and 19th centuries.

7Km
1:45

Leave the village heading east and just past the turning with the D193 turn right at the wayside cross. A little further on the GR turns right, crosses the D193 and goes back down into the valley. Cross the Noye and follow the path between the river and the railway. Cross over to the other bank at Hainneville and head south towards Chaussoy-Epagny-Hainneville church. Go round the church, turn right and you come to Chaussoy-Epagny.

CHAUSSOY-EPAGNY
✕ ⚓
18th century château.

7Km
1:45

Skirt the grounds of the château and head off right towards the Bois Planté and the Bois de Berny. The path turns right (spot height 84) and drops down to Berny-sur-Noye.

Berny-sur-Noye
15th century church.

2Km
0:30

As you leave the village the GR takes a path heading north-east towards Jumel.

JUMEL
🚌
(see map ref 8)
Junction with the GR123. The GR123 and GR124 take the same route as far as Estrées-sur-Noye. This section is also covered in Walk 3; see page 87.
Detour *15 mins*
AILLY-SUR-NOYE
🏠 ⛺ ✕ ￼ ⚓ 🚌 ⓔ

3Km
0:45

Follow the Rue Pasteur out of the village. Just after the shrine, leave the road and follow the path to the top of the hill. Walk along the side of a wood, the Bois de Beaumont, to reach Estrées-sur-Noye.

ESTRÉES-SUR-NOYE
🚌

When you come to the war memorial, the GR124 turns right. Just before you reach the

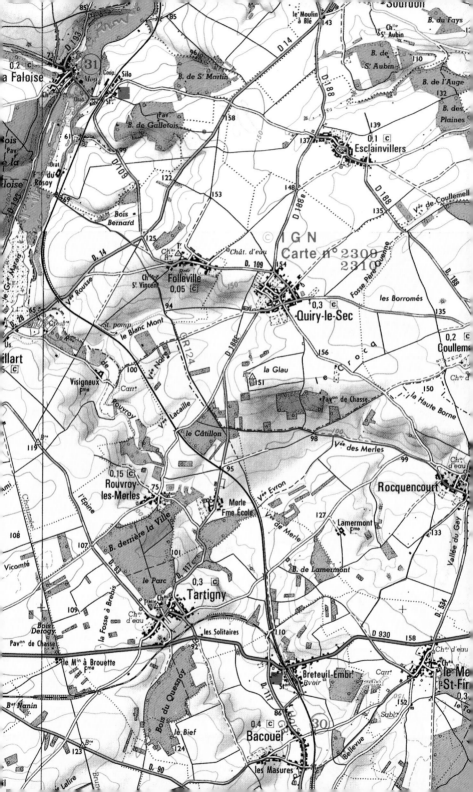

5Km
1:15

(see map ref 32)
Here the GR123 and GR124
split.
(see Walk 3, page 87, to
follow the GR123.)

COTTENCHY

16th century church.

3Km
0:45

LE PARACLET

(see map ref 33)
Remains of the old abbey of
Le Paraclet (now an
agricultural college); 18th
century abbey building;
oratory of Sainte-Ulphe.

4Km
1:00

BOVES

4Km
1:00

Bois de la Ville
(see map ref 35)
Junction with the GR124.
Detour *2 hrs 30 mins*
Amiens
(see map ref 34)

cemetery, turn left and go through a wood, the Bois du Roi. Take a right-angled bend (spot height 81) and walk down between the Bois du Roi and the Bois Monsieur. Further on the path runs beside the eastern edge of the Bois Monsieur and meets up with a path, onto which you turn right to cross the D75 to the west of Cottenchy.

The GR continues in the same direction and passes in front of the church. A little further on you cross a road and enter a wood, the Bois Magneux. Turn right to follow its northern edge. At the intersection turn left to come into Le Paraclet.

Alternative route From Le Paraclet to the Bois de la Ville via Boves. From the car park at Le Paraclet head north, pass close by the ruins of the château. When you reach the D167 turn right and go steeply downhill to Boves.

At the lights walk up to the railway station. Go under the bridge, turn right and follow a path which takes you away from the railway and climbs up to the Bois de la Ville.

Detour see left. When you leave Le Paraclet follow the same route as described in the alternative route above, as far as the D167 west of Boves. Turn left here for a few metres, then take a path on the right heading towards

---

Amiens is the administrative centre of the department of the Somme and the regional capital of Picardy. The cathedral of Notre-Dame is a masterpiece of pure Gothic art built when this style was at its height. It is one of the largest surviving religious buildings and the greatest of the Gothic cathedrals. Its statuary is known world-wide as are its 13th century recumbent bronze statues and above all its superb stalls dating from the end of the 15th century and the beginning of the 16th. Guided visits are available. To the east of the town are the *hortillonnages*, market gardens surrounded by water. You reach them in odd-looking boats, which are 9 metres long and have high prows.

Mont Henry. At the intersection (spot height 91), turn right onto a path going north-west, which leads to the football ground on the outskirts of Amiens.

As you leave Le Paraclet the GR124 turns right just past the oratory of Sainte-Ulphe. Before reaching the bridge turn left and follow the railway until you come to the D90. Turn left along the road, then, after the bridge over the River Avre, turn right and after passing the railway bridge follow the path up to cross the D935. Continue along the edge of a wood, the Bois de la Ville, where you join the alternative route from Boves. Cross the D934 and head north-east towards Gentelles.

Turn right along the D168 and at the cross-roads after the water tower turn left and continue until you come to the N29. Turn left and just after the bridge over the railway line take the road to the right. At the locality known as La Plaine de Lance turn right. At the third intersection turn left, heading north. Cross the D1 and carry straight on towards Aubigny.

From the village square at Aubigny drop down right towards the Somme. Turn right and continue beside it. Cross the bridge and you come to Corbie.

From the square in front of the abbey church the GR heads towards the railway station. Just past the footbridge over the railway, turn left and follow the road along the Ancre until you come to La Neuville.

Turn right onto the D30 and continue until you leave La Neuville. Take a road to the right passing the cemetery. About 1 kilometre after the pumping station (Station de pompage), turn up a path on the left. Skirt a wood, the

6Km
1:30

GENTELLES

Church rebuilt in 1920; 12th century font.

8Km
2:00

AUBIGNY

*(see map ref 36)
16th century church, much altered during the 19th century.*

2Km
0:30

CORBIE

Old Benedictine abbey founded in 657; church of Saint-Pierre; 14th century abbey-church rebuilt in the 18th century. Home of Sainte Colette (1381–1447), who reformed the three Orders of St Francis of Assissi.

1Km
0:15

LA NEUVILLE

Church dating from the beginning of the 16th century. Doorway has tympanum depicting Christ's

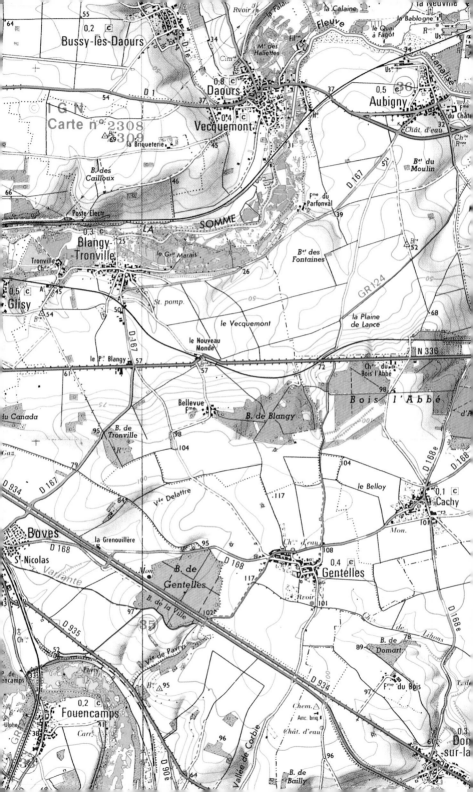

5Km
1:15

entry into Jerusalem on Palm Sunday. Frame and background are the walls and towers of the town of Corbie. Inside are some 14th century bas reliefs, and a 12th century font.

LAHOUSSOYE

4Km
1:00

18th century church.

Fréchencourt

5Km
1:15

*(see map ref 37)
19th century church; 19th century castle with parts that are older.*
Detour *45 mins*

BAVELINCOURT

MOLLIENS-AU-BOIS

2Km
0:30

16th century church; 19th century château with a chapel dating from 1760.

Mirvaux

3Km
0:45

16th century church; 12th century font.

HÉRISSART

7Km
2:45

RAINCHEVAL

4Km
1:00

19th century church; 18th century château.

Vauchelles-lès-Authie

Bois d'Escardonneuse, and join up with a road, which you follow to the left to reach Lahoussoye.

Go through the village and turn right at the cemetery. Turn left onto the D929 and 100 metres further on take the road on the right which runs alongside a wood, the Bois de Parmont. Cross the D115 and you come to Fréchencourt.

Go through the village of Fréchencourt and turn right to walk beside the château and then a wood, the Bois de Quesnoy. When you get to the end of the wood fork left. Cross the D919 and continue up a path running beside the Bois de Montigny and the Bois de Molliens to reach Molliens-au-Bois.

As you leave Molliens take the path which skirts the château on the right and drops down to Mirvaux.

Take the road opposite the church and turn right. At the bend in the road (spot height 91) carry straight on up a path until you get to an outcrop of sandstone. Turn right here and carry on until you come to Hérissart.

After passing Hérissart church fork left, then take the path on the left. Turn left onto the D114 and turn right along a path leading to a wood, the Bois de Quesnoy. Carry on in the same direction and cross the D23 at map ref 38. When you come to the Vallée Lupart, head left until you arrive at Raincheval.

As you leave the village, turn east along the D31, then take the road to the left leading into Vauchelles-lès-Authie.

The GR passes the church, crosses the D938

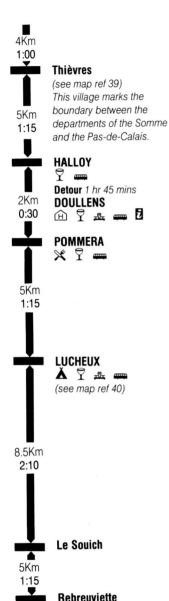

Thièvres
(see map ref 39)
This village marks the boundary between the departments of the Somme and the Pas-de-Calais.

HALLOY
♈ 🚌
Detour *1 hr 45 mins*
DOULLENS
🏨 ♈ 🚉 🚌 ℹ

POMMERA
✕ ♈ 🚌

LUCHEUX
▲ ♈ 🚉 🚌
(see map ref 40)

Le Souich

Rebreuviette
(see map ref 41)
Junction with the GR121.
Walk 1 continues along the GR121.

4Km 1:00
5Km 1:15
2Km 0:30
5Km 1:15
8.5Km 2:10
5Km 1:15

and continues opposite along a path which later crosses the D152 to reach Thièvres.

Turn right onto the D1 and after passing the church turn left. At the fork take the right-hand path going up past a wood, the Bois d'Orville. About 1 kilometre further on take the second path on the right, then the first on the left. Follow the D24 to the right to reach Halloy.

After passing the church, turn right onto the road which crosses the N25 and you come to Pommera.

After passing the cemetery take the path to the left heading towards a wood, the Bois de Watron. Follow a path along the valley bottom, then turn left along the course of a stream, which only flows periodically. Then follow the D200, which later joins the D5. Turn right onto this road and continue until you come to Lucheux.

Just before the cross as you come out of Lucheux, the GR turns right, comes to a small wood and skirts it to the north. Cross the River Grouche and at a crossroads turn right onto the D5 until you come to a path on the right. Follow this path towards the Chapelle Saint-Léger, and turn left to cross the D5 a little further on. Carry straight on along the path running along the eastern edge of the Forêt de Lucheux. Where the path meets a road, turn left and cross the northern part of the forest, crossing the Chemin Royal. On leaving the forest you reach Le Souich.

Just past the water tower, turn right along a path heading north until you reach Rebreuviette.

WALK 2

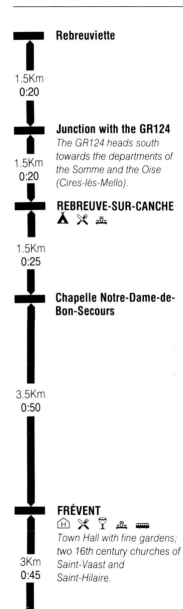

Rebreuviette

1.5Km
0:20

Junction with the GR124
*The GR124 heads south
towards the departments of
the Somme and the Oise
(Cires-lès-Mello).*

1.5Km
0:20

REBREUVE-SUR-CANCHE

1.5Km
0:25

**Chapelle Notre-Dame-de-
Bon-Secours**

3.5Km
0:50

FRÉVENT
*Town Hall with fine gardens;
two 16th century churches of
Saint-Vaast and
Saint-Hilaire.*

3Km
0:45

Follow the road D339 for 300 metres, then walk through the village along various streets to the left of this road until you come to a chapel on the corner of the Rue de L'Ancienne Gare, which marks the spot where the GR121 meets the GR124.

From the junction with the GR124 follow the GR121 towards the north and west through Rebreuviette to where it meets up with the D339 and crosses it at Rebreuve-sur-Canche.

In Rebreuve, turn right onto the D84 for a short distance in the direction of Honval, but leave it again at a bend in the road to climb a tarmac path going north-west overlooking the valley of the Canche. Pass by the chapel of Notre-Dame-de-Bon-Secours.

Turn left, going in a south westerly direction towards a path which drops steeply down to the road leading to the hamlet of Petit-Bouret. In front of the chapel go down to the left, heading south, until you reach the Canche. Do not cross, but follow the right-hand bank in a westerly direction, along a path through the meadows and bushes, following the way-marks. As you pass the grounds of the château of Cercamp, pick up a path which runs under some fine trees to join the road linking Frévent to the D339. Turn left onto this road for 25 metres, and taking a path on the right running beside some vegetable gardens, you will come to Frévent.

Follow the GR to the public gardens, once the grounds of the former château, overlooked by a little square. When you reach the square climb to the right up a tarmac path and continue as this becomes a track, crossing the hillside through pastures until you meet up with the D111. Turn left along this road in a south westerly direction until you come to the village of Ligny-sur-Canche.

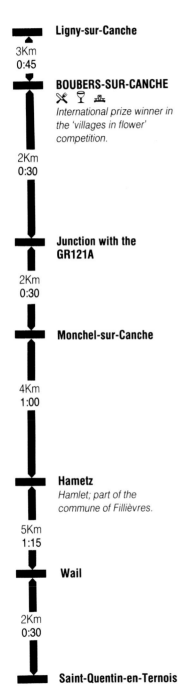

Ligny-sur-Canche

3Km
0:45

BOUBERS-SUR-CANCHE

International prize winner in the 'villages in flower' competition.

2Km
0:30

Junction with the GR121A

2Km
0:30

Monchel-sur-Canche

4Km
1:00

Hametz
Hamlet; part of the commune of Fillièvres.

5Km
1:15

Wail

2Km
0:30

Saint-Quentin-en-Ternois

Pass through the village in front of the church, then follow a farm track overlooking the river until you come to Boubers-sur-Canche.

Turn left as you come into the village and cross the square by the church; then turn left and cross the bridge over the Canche. Look at the flowers in the farmyard on the right, then follow a narrow road on the right as you leave the village. After that take a path on the right, cross the Canche over a narrow bridge and continue through the trees and meadows until you come to 'L'Enclos Annette', not far from a wood, the Bois de Boubers, where the GR121 joins up with the GR121A.

The GR121A called the 'Ternois path' heads north-east towards Saint-Pol-sur-Ternoise. To follow the Tour du Ternois, see page 63.

At the junction turn left following the GR121 and you will come to Monchel-sur-Canche.

In Monchel you will pass in front of the church and meet up with the D102. Turn left there along a by-road leading to Conchy-sur-Canche, which later becomes a farm track running along the hillside. Go past the cemetery of Aubrometz, where the path nears the Canche, but then head off away from the river once more, following the path as it climbs towards the chapel of Notre-Dame-du-Mont-Carmel in the hamlet of Hametz.

The GR passes through the hamlet along a road which brings you to the chapel of Notre-Dame-de-Bonne-Foi. Here you take a dirt track, which climbs up to higher ground then down again towards the river to the village of Wail.

After passing a wayside cross, you will come to the D98. Turn left along the road and follow the Canche. About 200 metres further on cross La Riviérette stream and continue on the D98 as far as the intersection with the D110, where you turn left to the hamlet of Saint-Quentin-en-Ternois.

Proceed through the hamlet, past the chapel

47

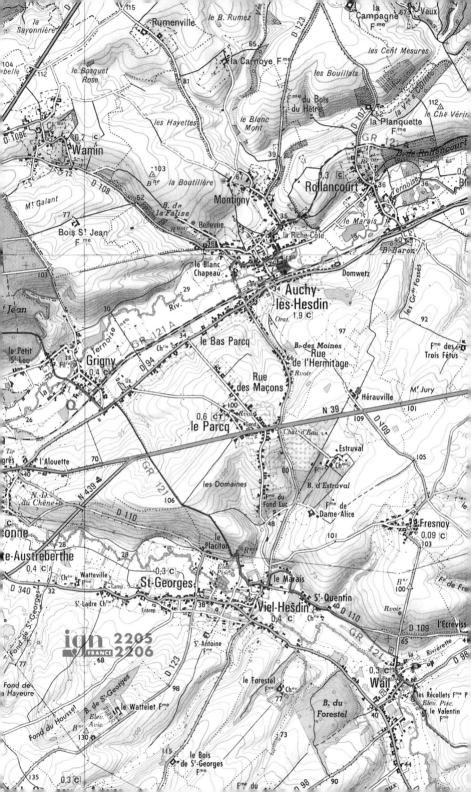

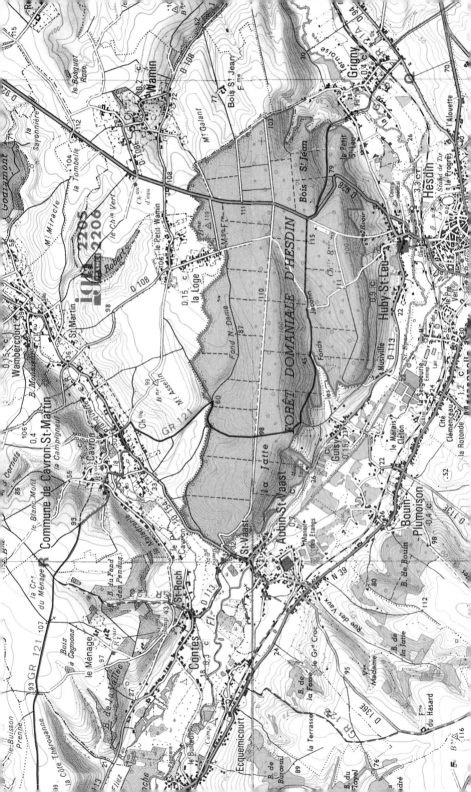

1Km
0:15

Vieil-Hesdin

4Km
1:00

Grigny
Where the GR121 meets the GR121A from Saint-Pol-sur-Ternoise. See page 73.

0.5Km
0:10

Petit-Saint-Leu
Detour *40 mins*
HESDIN
From Petit-Saint-Leu a road leads to Hesdin where you will find: Town Hall; old houses; church of Notre-Dame.

1Km
0:15

Forêt domaniale d'Hesdin

8Km
2:00

CAVRON-SAINT-MARTIN
Detour *1 hr*
AUBIN-SAINT-WAAST
Take the D154 (south-west) and continue on it when the GR121 branches right.

2Km
0:30

Junction with the GR123
The GR123 heads left in a southerly direction towards Carlepont.

7Km
1:45

of Sainte-Colette, then a fish farm and along the edge of a wood, veer right to take the road around the Marais, which then brings you back to the D110. Turn right to come to Vieil-Hesdin.

Walk past the church continuing along the D110 and as you go round a bend take a path on the right climbing north-west up to higher ground, finally coming to the N39. On the other side of the N39 continue down a path to the D94. Turn left onto the D94 for 200 metres and then turn along a road which crosses a level crossing and will bring you to Grigny.

The GR121 crosses a footbridge over the River Ternoise and climbs straight on up a path to bring you to the hamlet of Petit-Saint-Leu.

From the hamlet of Saint-Leu continue along the GR to the south-eastern edge of the Forêt domaniale d'Hesdin (Hesdin State Forest).

Go through the forest in a westerly then a north westerly direction. When you come out of the forest, use the farm track running along the side of the hill (Mont Asselin) to drop down to a chapel and take a by-road into Cavron-Saint-Martin.

The route through the village forks several times so be careful to follow the waymarks. After crossing the River Planquette, climb the path to higher ground and carry on until you come to a small valley, where the GR121 meets the GR123.

Following the GR121 towards the west, you pass by the Croix du Ménage and join a made-up path. Turn right at the fork to pick up the made-up path leading to the D113, which it follows for 300 metres. After the bridge, turn

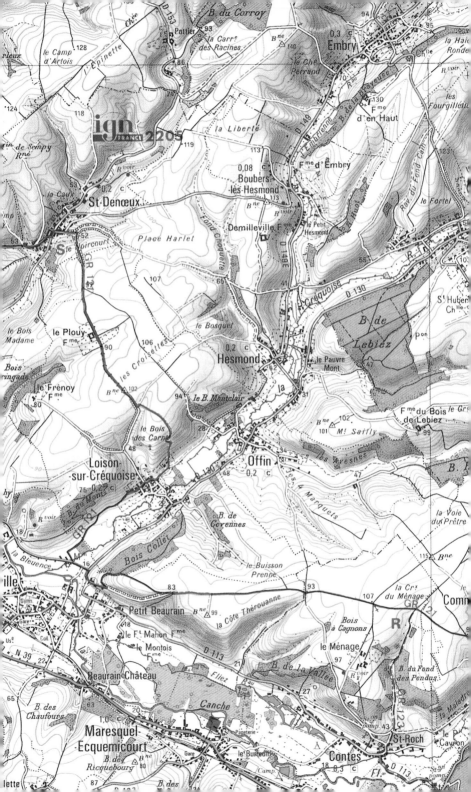

right on to a farm track leading to Loison-sur-Créquoise.

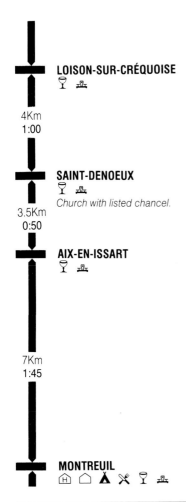

LOISON-SUR-CRÉQUOISE

4Km
1:00

After passing through the village of Loison-sur-Créquoise, follow a made-up farm track on the left. Bear left at the fork and then right towards Le Plouy farm. Carry straight on and turn left at the junction to reach the D153. Following the D153 round to the left you come to Saint-Denoeux.

SAINT-DENOEUX

Church with listed chancel.

3.5Km
0:50

Continue westwards on the D149 as far as spot height 93 on the map. Take the tarmac farm track on the right, which cuts across the Chaussée Brunehaut (old Roman road) and you come to Aix-en-Issart.

AIX-EN-ISSART

7Km
1:45

After going through the village of Aix-en-Issart, in the direction of Montcavrel, take a grassy path on the left, which climbs up to Mont Bart. Where the paths cross, follow the GR121 left onto the farm track leading to Vitrouval farm and you will come to a narrow road that drops down west to the Chartreuse. At the cross roads, after the cemetery, turn right onto the D113 until you reach Neuville-sous-Montreuil. At the crossroads in the centre of the village turn left in the direction of Montreuil and cross the N1. Cross the River Canche and then a level crossing. Follow the GR121 as it turns right up a street which brings you to the Chemin de la Citadelle at Montreuil.

MONTREUIL

The GR climbs to the right, following a picturesque walk round the promontory the

---

Montreuil

An old fortified town, Montreuil has retained most of its brick walls dating from the 13th, 16th and 17th centuries. The citadel, with towers dating from the 13th century, houses a collection of gemstones. The church of Saint-Saulve has a nave with parts dating from the 12th, 13th and 16th centuries, a doorway in the Flamboyant style, 13th century tombs and a collection of precious objects.

Montreuil used to be on the coast — Montreuil-sur-Mer — before the Marguenterre existed. To the south, chalk plateaux. To the north, the Canche valley and the high plateaux, and to the west. . .

Again we meet the high chalk plateaux with their covering of plateau silt (which makes good growing soil) and their open fields of commercial crops. This plateau is intersected by such rivers as the Course and the Dordogne.

town is built on. It passes through a tunnel and a gate in the ramparts and drops down again through grazing land to the road.

5Km
1:15

Turn right and go south to join the D139. On the other side of the road take a tarred farm track which climbs up to higher ground. The GR goes past a farm and a little further on bears right towards the D146. Turn right onto the D146 in a northerly direction and you will come to La Calotterie.

la Calotterie

The path heads east through the village. Further on it strikes north, taking a road to the left which crosses an area of ditches and streams. Go through the hamlets of Basse Flaque and Visemarest. Leave Hurtebise farm on the left and turn right onto the D145, continuing northwards until you reach the N39. Turn right here for 300 metres, take the D146 on the left, go over a level crossing in the hamlet of Enocq, then turn right to cross the River Dordogne and, following a farm track, you will arrive at Bréxent-Enocq.

7.5Km
1:50

BRÉXENT-ENOCQ

The GR passes through the village along a road running parallel to the D146 and joins up with it at spot height 15 on the map. Turn left along the D146 in a northerly direction for 400 metres and then turn right along a farm track, heading east towards the south-western edge of the Bois de Longvillers (private wood). Before reaching the wood bear left (north-north-east) along a farm track climbing up to Longueroye farm. Continue to spot height 108 on the map. Here you join a narrow road. Turn right on to this and walk east until you come to the N1 opposite Cabaret à Leu farm. Turn left on to this road and 150 metres further on turn right onto the D147 and continue eastwards until you reach Bernieulles.

6Km
1:30

BERNIEULLES

Petite Randonée (short distance) footpaths in the vicinity are signposted.

Detour *30 mins*

BEUSSENT

Opposite the church in Bernieulles the GR121 turns left onto the D147E. After 300 metres, you leave it to take a path on the right, which heads north towards Fernehem Farm, then climbs up to higher ground, where it turns right onto the D148 in an easterly direction. After a wide right-hand bend to the right, turn left, pass by the Bois d'Enguinehaut, then head

6Km
1:30

At Petit-Inxent there is a horseriding centre for the Val de Course. From Bernieulles follow the D147 south-east.

due north towards Thubeauville.

Thubeauville

At the centre of the village a by-road on the left takes you through the valleys to the hamlet of Sequières. (About 5 kilometres to the north is Samer, where you will find a full range of supplies). To the west of the village take a farm track climbing north towards a high voltage power line until you come to a path intersection.

3Km
0:45

Path intersection
Situated to the south-west of Mont-Corbeau. From this point a path runs off to join the GR120 near a place called Fort Manoir, to the east of Samer. See Walk 5, Tour du Boulonnais, page 175.

Do not go under the high voltage power line. Instead, turn left at the intersection, following the path known as Le Chemin du Bois de L'Eperche, which brings you to the junction of the N1 with the D125. You then cross a wood, the Bois de Tingry, which is private property, and at the point where the high voltage power line leaves the road bear right and head north-west along a farm track running beside the power line. After crossing the D239 you come to Haut-Pichot.

5Km
1:15

Haut-Pichot

In Haut-Pichot you follow the road through the village and take a farm track on the left which branches off in a north-westerly direction towards Mont Violette (176 metres), then drops down to the D215, which it crosses to reach the hamlet of Pelincthun. Follow a narrow road, then turn right to head north-west to the hamlet of La Neuville.

3.5Km
0:50

LA NEUVILLE

Leaving La Neuville, go under a bridge and then turn right in the direction of the forest to follow the scenic route, which after crossing the D940, brings you to the silence of the Hardelot State Forest. At this point you reach a family guest house, called Golfers-Hôtel.

4.5Km
1:05

GOLFERS-HÔTEL

Turn right along the road leading to the château d'Hardelot. Then turn left and continue along the road until you come to a turning on the right, the Chemin des Juifs, constructed by Jewish prisoners during the occupation and which joins the coastal path.

4Km
1:00

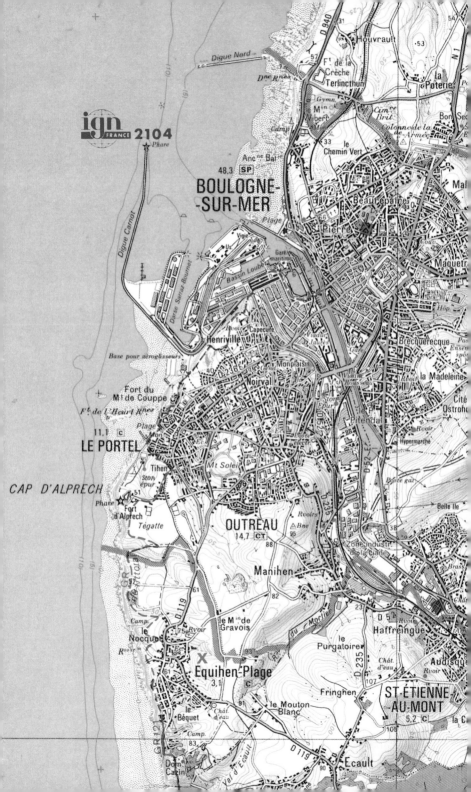

Hardelot State Forest

Here, just before reaching the coast, walkers enter the Hardelot State Forest, an area rich in wildlife, with distant views of the cliffs, dunes, marshes, mud flats and estuaries, which make the coast between Gravelines and Boulogne so varied and interesting.

The 130 metres Cap Blanc-Nez is composed mainly of chalk and was formed at a time when the Continent was covered by sea. Now that it is above sea level, it is subject to constant erosion by the waves. Cap Griz-Nez (49 metres) is a headland of grey slate and yellow sandstone jutting out into the Channel. It is the nearest point to England and has a lighthouse.

The dunes form a natural barrier which protects the coastal strip from flooding. Strenuous efforts have been made to protect them; in fact the Conservatoire du Littoral (a society for the protection of the coast) has bought nearly 2,000 hectares of dunes to protect them from developers, to restore them and to open them gradually to the public. The coastal path passes Slack and Aval dunes, which are in the process of being restored and goes through the less threatened areas of the Sangatte-Blériot and Platier d'Oye dunes.

The dunes isolate the marshes on their landward side from the sea. These marshes, areas regularly flooded by rainwater running off the land, are covered in parts by extensive reedbeds and attract many animals and birds which go there to escape predators and to breed. The Marais of Tardinghen, bordered by the Aval and Châtelet dunes, covers the site of the old port of Wissant.

Coastal path
Detour *40 mins*
HARDELOT-PLAGE

4Km
1:00
Walk along the coastal path.

9Km
2:15

EQUIHEN-PLAGE

BOULOGNE-SUR-MER

The GR121 continues north through the dunes along the coastal path. It cuts across a narrow access road from Ecault to the sea and a little further on, as the Cazin estate comes into view (intermittently waymarked), you reach the road running along beside the sea leading to a place known as the Barque Renversée in the district of Equihen-Plage.

If you follow the GR121 along the coast northwards you can reach Boulogne. (See the route marked on page 61.)

GR121A
TOUR DU TERNOIS

The GR121A or Tour du Ternois is an alternative to the direct GR121 route between Boubers-sur-Canche (page 47) and Grigny (page 51).

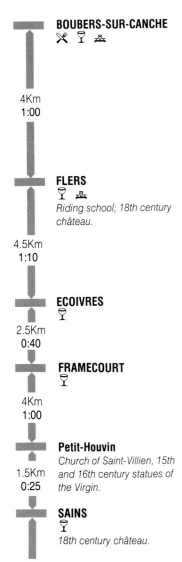

BOUBERS-SUR-CANCHE

4Km
1:00

FLERS

Riding school; 18th century château.

4.5Km
1:10

ECOIVRES

2.5Km
0:40

FRAMECOURT

4Km
1:00

Petit-Houvin
Church of Saint-Villien, 15th and 16th century statues of the Virgin.

1.5Km
0:25

SAINS
18th century château.

As you leave the village follow the GR121 for 1.5 kilometres until you come to a wood, the Bois de Boubers. Here the GR121A heads north-east, away from the GR121. Take the dirt track along the edge of the wood opposite the sign 'GR du Ternois'. About 1.5 kilometres further on you go through a gap made in the fence, cross a meadow to the edge of the wood once more, and turn right along a track which comes to the D109. Turn left here until you reach Flers.

Before you reach the château at Flers, leave the D109 and follow a road on the right going north-east, which will bring you to the junction with the D103, to the east of Flamermont. At the junction take the path on the right crossing the Plaine d'Ecoivres. When you come to a road turn left, cross the D104 and then you will come to Ecoivres.

You do not go through the village of Ecoivres, but instead follow a dirt track which skirts it and heads towards a water tower situated on the edge of Framecourt.

Before Framecourt, turn right along the D916 from Frévent to Saint-Pol for 30 metres, then turn left. About 800 metres further on turn sharply to the left, taking the first path across the fields, which leads to Petit-Houvin.

In the hamlet pick up the D103, following it as far as the railway line from Saint-Pol to Frévent. Cross the Fond de Sains along a narrow made-up road in the direction of Epainchen.

As you come into the hamlet, turn down a path lined by tall trees, which goes a little way downhill and then enters a wood, the Bois de Sains. Follow the dirt track by a hunting lodge.

2Km
0:30

Ocoche

1.5Km
0:30

Tachincourt

2Km
0:30

Epainchen
Hamlet in the district of Roëllecourt. At Roëllecourt there is a 16th century church with an inscription dated 1620.

2Km
0:30

While still in the wood turn right, then walk beside the wood and, finally, when you are down on the flat, follow a farm track until you get to the D23. Pick up the path again on the opposite side of the road and continue to Ocoche.

Walk through the hamlet. At the first cross-roads carry straight on until you come to Tachincourt.

Leaving Tachincourt, turn left onto the D85 for 250 metres, then turn onto a dirt track. This track, known as the Chemin des Morts, runs alongside a wood, the Bois d'Epainchen, then crosses undulating terrain to meet up with a narrow made-up road which drops down to Epainchen.

Cross the Arras–Boulogne railway line and the N39 following a narrow road. Turn left onto a dirt track, which further on becomes a narrow road; then turn right on to a track running alongside the meadows which are the source of the Ternoise. At the Auberge de Catherinette, turn left along the D85E for 300 metres, then turn right onto a dirt track, which runs along-side the Bois Saint-Michel and leads to the church of Saint-Michel-sur-Ternoise.

Val de la Sensée

SAINT-MICHEL-SUR-TERNOISE

△ ✕ ♉ ♨ ☷

1.5Km
0:25

SAINT-POL-SUR-TERNOISE

⌂ ✕ ♉ ♨ ♞ ☷

Junction with the Link path from Bours on the GR127 and the GR121A — Rue d'Aire and Rue de Conteville.

4Km
1:00

HERNICOURT

△ ♉ ♨ ☷

Beautiful view over the valley of the Ternoise.
To reach the camping site beside the Ternoise turn left to go down to the village.

3Km
0:45

MONCHY-CAYEUX

✕ ♉ ♨ ☷

Château dating from the 15th and 16th centuries.

2Km
0:30

ANVIN

⌂ ✕ ♉ ♨ ♞ ☷

'Village of flowers'; 15th century church; two mills.

Walk down a made-up road until you come to the N39, turn right along the N39, go under the railway bridge and bear right towards the Faubourg d'Arras. About 500 metres further on, turn right into a narrow road leading to the Mont de Saint-Pol (military cemetery), then go down the road to the Faubourg de Béthune. Walking down the Rue de Béthune you arrive in the centre of Saint-Pol-sur-Ternoise.

Cross the Rue de Béthune to head in the direction of Troisvaux. About 250 metres further on, turn left into a side street which leads to the Rue d'Aire. Take this in the direction of Cauchain-Verloingt. After passing a chapel turn right, leaving the village behind you on the left. Take a path across the hillside through undulating terrain covered by vegetation, until you come to a spot overlooking the Ternoise at the village of Hernicourt.

Cross the road and pick up a dirt track. About 1 kilometre further on cross another road (if you turn left here you get back to Hernicourt) and continue straight on through land belonging to the district of Wavrans-sur-Ternoise until you reach the hamlet of Saint-Martin. Here there is a very beautiful view of the village down in the valley. Turn left along the D99 for 200 metres, then turn right at the school and cross a stream. Go up the road for 300 metres and then head left in the direction of the church, which overlooks the Ternoise valley. At the top of the hill, turn left onto a dirt track, which follows the Ternoise valley along the hillside until it comes to the fish farm of Monchy-Cayeux.

Continue along the hillside on a narrow made-up road. About 1 kilometre further on, turn left onto a dirt track, which may have been ploughed over, to join the D70. Turn left here for 1 kilometre, then pick up a disused railway line on the left and cross a bridge to come to Anvin.

Follow the D343 in the direction of Saint-Pol as far as the crossroads at the edge of town, where you will find a small chapel. At this point take a path to the right running beside the

67

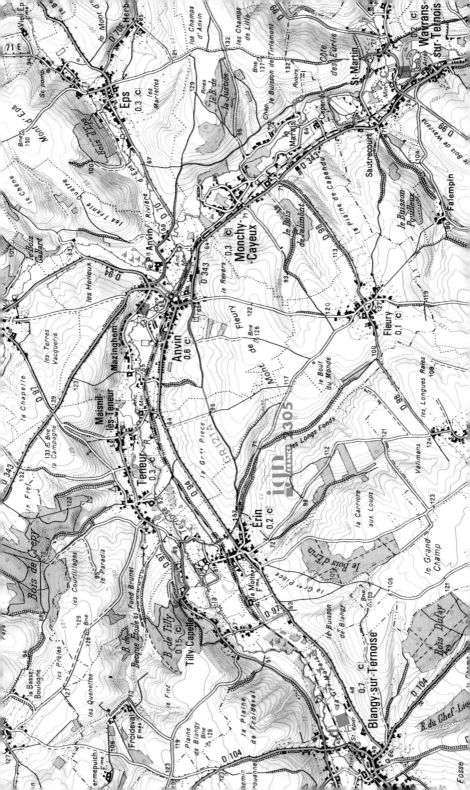

3.5Km
0:50

ERIN

3Km
0:45

Tilly-Capelle

2Km
0:30

BLANGY-SUR-TERNOISE

Buildings of the old abbey (1771): church with 17th century door.

3.5Km
0:50

Blingel

2.5Km
0:40

ROLLANCOURT

2Km
0:30

Very beautiful view of the valley of the Ternoise.

AUCHY-LES-HESDIN

cemetery and follow it for 3 kilometres. Half way along this path you may find it is under cultivation for a distance of 500 metres or so. in which case cross the fields carefully; you are allowed to cross. You then come to Erin.

Before Erin bear right onto a path and cross the D94, the railway, and a footbridge over the Ternoise. Turn left along a made-up path, cross the D97 and follow a footpath, which runs alongside the Bois de Tilley and drops down to Tilley-Capelle.

At the junction with the D97 turn right along a road heading south-west towards the intersection with the D104, which leads to Blangy-sur-Ternoise.

The GR does not go through Blangy; instead it crosses the D104 and continues straight on for 500 metres, then turns right in the direction of a wood, the Bois de l'Abbaye. As it climbs it overlooks the valley. Later on it drops down towards the Bois de Courcelle and joins another road at the hamlet of Courcelle, which is administratively part of Blingel.

The GR does not go through the village of Blingel; it leaves the road where this bends to the left. Continue straight on, then turn right and follow a narrow track which climbs steeply towards a wood, the Bois de Rollancourt. At the top of the hill turn left, walk beside the wood for 200 metres, then follow the path into the wood. There is a game-keeper's house on the right, where you come out of the wood at the intersection with the D107, and where, if you turn left, the road takes you to Rollancourt.

To continue on the GR, do not go through the village, but cross the D107 and take a dirt track along the hillside.

About 1 kilometre further on take a track to the left, which first of all slopes down gently and then steeply to arrive at the D123 which brings you to Auchy-les-Hesdin.

In the town follow the D123 until you come to the main square, then follow the D108 in the

71

4Km
1:00

Very fine abbey-church built between 1150 and 1250, altered in 1611. Organs; Van Dyck painting; wood panelling.

Grigny

The path meets the GR121 near the level-crossing. See page 51.

direction of Wamin. At the football ground, turn left along the road leading to Le Parcq. Before you reach the level-crossing turn right along a path running beside the Arras-to-Boulogne railway line until you come to Grigny.

If you turn right the GR121 takes you to the village of Boulogne; turn left and you come to Vieil-Hesdin and Arras.

From Grigny it is 18 kilometres to Boubers via the GR121, which completes the round trip of the Tour du Ternois. This route is described in reverse in Walk 2, pages 47 and 51.

WALK 3

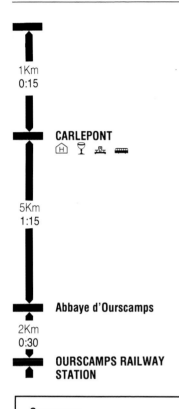

1Km
0:15

CARLEPONT

5Km
1:15

Abbaye d'Ourscamps

2Km
0:30

**OURSCAMPS RAILWAY
STATION**

The waymarks for the GR123 path start in the woods, on the GR12A, to the north-east of Tracy-le-Mont and to the south of Carlepont. See map ref 1. Leaving the GR12A, which heads north-east towards Caisnes, the GR123 bears left, leaves the wood, runs by the side of a sports ground and arrives at Carlepont.

The GR goes down the street on the left in the direction of the hamlet of Huleu. As you leave the built-up area take a path on the left leading to a wood, the Bois Leblond. When you come to an intersection (spot height 48), turn to the right onto a straight path until you come to the D165. Turn right here until you come to a small bridge. Then turn left and head north-west along a path which, on leaving the forest, the Forêt d'Ourscamps, joins up with the D48. Follow this road until you come to the Abbaye d'Ourscamps.

Still following the D48, cross the River Oise and the Canal du Nord to reach the railway station at Ourscamps.

After passing the railway bridge turn right onto the D535 and carry on until you come to Chiry-

---

Ourscamps

A Cistercian abbey founded in 1129 on land belonging to Simon de Vermandois, the Bishop of Noyon, who, according to an ancient text, 'was so weighed down by the burdens of office that he wanted monks to pray for him to help him bear them' that St Bernard sent twelve monks from the Abbey of Clairvaux. The name gave rise to a legend by a play on words. It is said that in the middle of the 7th century St Eloi, minister of Dagobert and Bishop of Noyon, built an oratory and set up a community, which at times he liked to retreat to. Some oxen were pulling a cart loaded with stones for the building of the chapel when a bear came out of the nearby forest and ate one of them. This made St Eloi so angry that he made the animal take the place of the ox in the team. The place was given the name Champ (camp in the dialect of Picardy) de l'Ours (Field of the Bear). In 1490 the abbey received the relic of the head of St Anne. It became a place of pilgrimage and the centre from which the cult of St Anne spread throughout France. In 1948 the Order of the Servants of Jesus and Mary, devoted to the preaching of the Gospel to young people, was established there.

1.5Km
0:20 *(see map ref 2)*

Ourscamps.

CHIRY-OURSCAMPS

Entering Chiry-Ourscamps, cross the N32 and go up the street opposite, past the camping site, to the junction with the GR de Pays du Noyonnais.

Junction
On the right, a local footpath, the Tour du Noyonnais, takes walkers on a tour of the area around Noyon.

The GR123 takes a path to the left going along the side of Mont Conseil. A little further on, on your left, you pass the yellow and red markers for another local footpath, the GR de Pays du Compiègnois, a tour of the area around Compiègne.

The GR climbs north-west along a valley bottom as far as the intersection known as the Cinq Piliers, an old quarry in which there is an archway of roughly hewn stone with 5 pillars, on which German soldiers carved their motto during the First World War.

5Km
1:15

Take a narrow path on the left above the quarry. Further on you come to a spot where 5 paths meet. Follow the one to the left. About 100 metres further on take a path on the right down into a clearing. Then walk along the edge of the wood until you reach a narrow road. Turn left along the road until you come to Orval.

GR de Pays de Compiègnois
(The Compiègne footpath)
This route, linking the GR123 and the GR124A, and making use of several other long-distance footpaths, makes a round trip of about 100 kilometres. The main stages along the route are:
● GR123, from the railway station at Ourscamps to Chiry-Ourscamps;
● GR de Pays: Montagne d'Attiche, Chevincourt, Melicocq, Coudun, Baugy, Ferme des Septvoies, Montplaisir, Mont d'Huette, Jonquières;
● GR124: from le Bocquet-Haut (Le Meux) to the Acaste intersection;
● GR12: from the Acaste intersection to Pierrefonds;
● GR12A: from Pierrefonds to Carlepont;
● GR123: from Carlepont to the railway station at Ourscamps.
Short walks between railway stations taking just one day are also possible.
● from Ourscamps to Choisy-au-Bac (24 kilometres);
● from Choisy-au-Bac to La Meux-Lacroix-St-Ouen (25 kilometres).

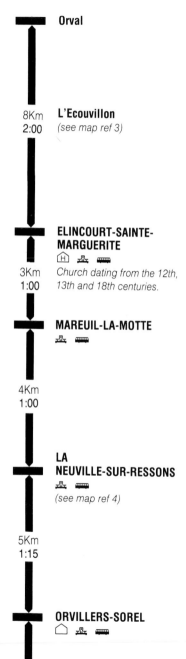

Orval

As you come into Orval the GR takes a road to the left, then turns right along a dirt path leding to a wayside cross (Croix Vignon), and then to a spring. You then take a path on the left that climbs up to the D57. Cross the D57 and take the road opposite leading to L'Ecouvillon.

8Km
2:00

L'Ecouvillon
(see map ref 3)

As you head south-west out of l'Ecouvillon (spot height 179), turn right onto a wide path going through a wood, the Bois de Thiescourt. Pass by a hunting-lodge and cross a cultivated clearing. The GR goes down the Montagne de Géremy and as it comes out of the wood follows a path heading off to the right to Elincourt-Sainte-Marguerite.

ELINCOURT-SAINTE-MARGUERITE

3Km
1:00

Church dating from the 12th, 13th and 18th centuries.

From the square in front of the church climb a path through a wood, the Bois de la Montagne du Couvent. At the end of the wood turn left towards the Montagne du Hazoir, then follow the path down to the right until you come to Mareuil-la-Motte.

MAREUIL-LA-MOTTE

4Km
1:00

Near the church at the western end of Mareuil-la-Motte the GR crosses the D78 and follows a dirt track almost opposite heading north-west. Follow the edge of a wood, the Bois de Ricquebourg, passing several paths leading off to the right. Further on turn right to head north along a path overlooking the valley (Vallée du Matz), then turn left and go through the village of La Neuville-sur-Ressons.

LA NEUVILLE-SUR-RESSONS

(see map ref 4)

5Km
1:15

As you leave Neuville-sur-Ressons the GR heads west along a road which crosses a railway and the Nord motorway. At the edge of a wood, the Bois du Roi David, take a path on the right which winds through old orchards until it comes to the corner of the wall of the Château de Sorel. At the next intersection, where a path on the left leads to the Château de Sorel where you can find accommodation, follow the road opposite until you come to Orvillers-Sorel.

ORVILLERS-SOREL

When you enter Orvillers-Sorel, take the first street on the right, then the first on the left to reach the N17. Turn right here for a few metres, then take the first path on the left, which a little further on (spot height 90) turns

Buildings in rural Picardy

The richness of the natural environment in Picardy is matched by the variety and quality of its architectural heritage, whether archaeological, as for example in the farms built by people who lived in the Somme basin in pre-Roman and Roman times, historical or rural. In spite of two world wars, there are many listed buildings in Picardy.

But perhaps what is most immediately striking is the way in which the shapes, materials and colours of traditional rural buildings fit in with their surroundings.

The farms in the region are particularly interesting. More than just simple dwellings, they form groups of dwellings or buildings in themselves that are quite different from the villages. In some areas they are arranged around enclosed courtyards, as on the plateau of Picardy and around Noyon or Soissons, and in others they form courtyards opening onto the road as in the Thiérache, the area around the towns of Guise, Vervins and Le Fère.

Although there are differences of style, rural buildings in Picardy resemble each other in general outline: their steeply sloping roofs, the shape of their walls and chimneys and the predominance of slate, roughcasting, brick and light materials.

4Km
1:00

BOULOGNE-LA-GRASSE
🏕 ⛺ 🚌
Detour 20 mins
CONCHY-LES-POTS
🏠 ✕

In Boulogne-La-Grasse turn right along the D27 and cross the N17 to reach the church of Conchy-les-Pots.

4Km
1:00

ONVILLERS
🍷 ⛺

2Km
0:30

right. When you come to the fork continue in the same (northerly) direction. Cross a small valley and, further on, take a path on the left coming from a farm, the Ferme du Moulin. When you come to a wayside cross turn right to come into Boulogne-la-Grasse.

The GR crosses the D27 into Boulogne-La-Grasse. At a junction turn left along the street that leads to the church. Go up to the right, then turn left and carry on until you see the ruins of the château. Turn left there and carry on to the water tower, where you take a path on the right along the side of a wood.

Further on, the path drops quite steeply to a dirt road which you follow to the left. When you come to the D524 turn right, then take the second path on the left along the side of a wood. Keeping to the field, you come to a wide path which heads right and brings you to Onvillers.

You leave Onvillers along a road heading west, then take the first path on the right. Pass a farm, the Ferme Houssoy, then take the second path on the left to the D68, where you turn right to get to Remaugies.

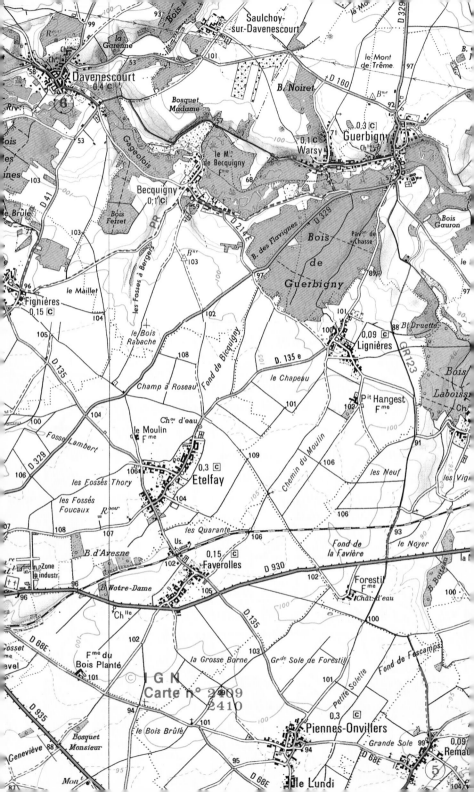

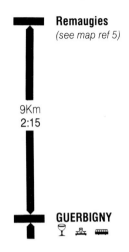

Remaugies
(see map ref 5)

9Km
2:15

GUERBIGNY

The GR follows the main street out of Remaugies. As you come to the last houses there is a fork. Turn left onto a path, which is tarred at this point, but further on is gravel. When you reach a copse turn sharp left along a path; then take the first path on the right and pass by a farm, the Ferme Forestil. Cross the D930 and the railway and continue in the same direction until you get to a road. Follow this in the same direction until it bends left, at which point you leave it and carry on in the same direction along a dirt track. You pass a pumping station, then turn left along the D68 to the centre of Guerbigny.

In the centre of the village, turn sharp left towards Warsy. Pass through this village and

The Somme

A coastline of chalk cliffs and sandy beaches, a countryside of plains and pastures, scrub and forest, rivers and lakes, the department of the Somme is a neatly woven patchwork. Prehistoric and Gallo-Roman sites, buildings in the Gothic style and reminders of military campaigns throughout the ages, all tell us of the rich and eventful history of this area, which has so often been at the centre of events in France, not least through war and occupation.

Many waterways cross the area, wending their way through green fertile valleys. The thick deposits of silt and the gentle gradients cause the rivers to meander, forming, as in the upper reaches of the Somme, many loops with curiously shaped oxbow lakes. The Somme has 4000 hectares of lakes and ponds. Surrounded by marsh and poplar, they provide a wonderful natural habitat for animal and bird life.

In places, as at Long or Suzanne, châteaux are reflected in the waters, and at Amiens, built on the banks of the Somme, the winding course of the river as it flows through the town has formed a patchwork of gardens where the *hortillons* (market gardeners) go about their business in boats. There, reflected in the waters, is that masterpiece of Gothic art, the cathedral, overlooking the old quarter of Saint-Leu, which once hummed with the activity of workshops.

The plateaux are very different from the more enclosed and secluded areas of wetland and woodland. Areas of large-scale farming, they are still rich in contrasts. The eastern part, the 'Santerre', with its even contours, is taken up by big farms, with open geometrically shaped fields, and, in places, huge farm buildings or huddled villages.

To the west of Amiens the appearance of these plateaux changes markedly. Lines of trees become more numerous and the terrain more undulating. Villages built of brick are replaced by farm buildings with cob walls, fodder and silage crops are grown more widely, and orchards are smaller and less geometrical in outline. The vegetation of the woods and the chalk hillsides, known here as *larris*, dot the countryside with green.

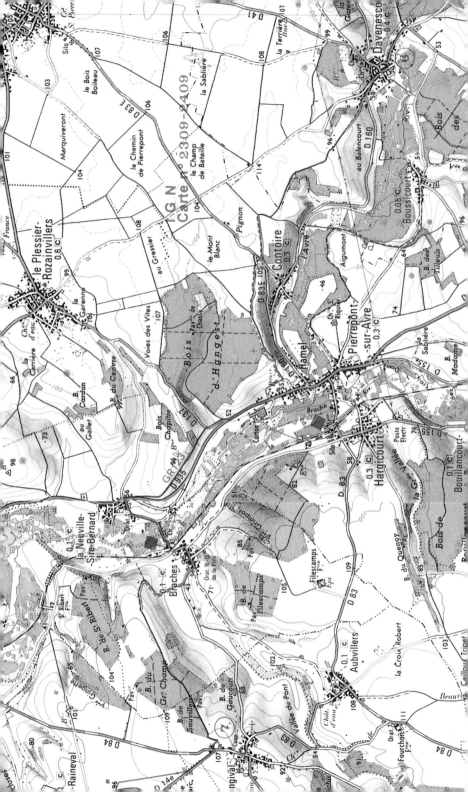

5Km
1:15

Church dating from the 13th and 15th centuries; 15th century chancel; font dating from 1567; several walls of the old castle remain.

continue along the valley to Davenscourt.

DAVENSCOURT

🍷 🚉 🚌

(see map ref 5)
Inside the church, built in the flamboyant style, there are 14th-century tombs, oak stalls, a lectern dating from 1685, a pulpit dating from 1720, and a 'Renaissance' font. Château dating from the end of the 18th century in extensive grounds. To the right of the gateway is a chapel, built in 1762, with a finely carved door.

6Km
1:30

The GR leaves Davenscourt along the D160 heading north-west. At the second fork take the path going up to the right, go under a power line and after passing a wood, turn right then left to reach the D83E above Contoire (café). Cross this road near two barns and take a path heading west along the side of a wood, the Bois d'Hangest. Drop down to Hamel and Pierrepont.

HAMEL ET PIERREPONT

✗ 🍷 🚉 🚂

3Km
0:50

Just before you come to the village the GR turns right, then immediately left to meet the D935. Turn right here and when you come to a fork turn right along the D137 for a few metres; then turn left onto a dirt track running parallel to the D935. You now come to La Neuville-Sire-Bernard.

LA NEUVILLE-SIRE-BERNARD

🍷 🚉

1.5Km
0:20

Follow the D935 for 50 metres, then take the first road on the left to Braches.

Braches

6Km
1:30

After going over the level crossing turn left, then twice to the right to go up a track along the edge of the Bois du Grand Champ. Take the path into this wood and continue through to the Bois de Sauvillers. As you come out of this wood turn left, then right, and cross the D84 to the north of Sauvillers-Mongival.

Sauvillers-Mongival
(see map ref 7)

Follow the D14E north-west, then turn right onto a grassy track. Further along bear left and you come to Mailly-Raineval.

Mailly-Raineval
Ruins of the old château belonging to the comte de Mailly.

At the centre of the village the GR takes a street on the right leading to the church, crosses the D14 and continues opposite along a narrow road in the direction of Rouvrel. Walk

85

7Km
1:45

along the edge of a wood, the Bois du Bellois. When you reach the second small valley turn left along the path up the Vallée Jean-Midi. Cross the D134 and you come to Ailly-sur-Noye.

AILLY-SUR-NOYE

🏠 ⛺ ✕ 🍷 🚂 🚌 🛈

Inside the 19th-century church there is a 15th century tomb in black stone of Jean de Luxembourg, Lord of Haubordin, and of his wife Jacqueline de la Trémouille. Above this sepulchre is a bas-relief in the form of a triptych dating from 1684, representing, in the centre Christ on the Cross, on the right St Martin of Tours, the patron saint of the church, and on the left St John the Baptist, patron saint of the donor. Also inside the church are a 15th century Ecco Homo and a curious hexagonally shaped font.

In Ailly, turn left along the D920, pass in front of the church and head down the main street. Cross the river Noye to reach Jumel.

1.5Km
0:20

JUMEL

*(see map ref 8)
Junction with the GR124.*

The GR123 and GR124 follow the same route as far as Éstrées-sur-Noye. This section is also covered in Walk 1; see page 29.

3Km
0:45

Climb some steps opposite the war memorial, skirt the church and take the Rue Pasteur out of the village. Just past the shrine leave the road and head north-west along a tarmac path climbing up to the higher ground. Walk along the edge of a wood, the Bois de Beaumont, and you come to Estrées-sur-Noye.

ESTRÉES-SUR-NOYE

🚌

This village owes its name to the Roman road which linked Lutetia (Paris) to Samarobriva (Amiens).

Here the GR123 and the GR124 split, the GR124 going off in a north-easterly direction towards Corbie. (See Walk 1, page 29, to follow the GR124.)

8Km
2:0

The GR takes the path on the left leading to the water tower. Cross the D7 and follow the path opposite, heading south-west. Later turn right and cross an area of conifer scrub. At the

top of the hill, in sight of the village of Oresmaux, turn right along a path leading towards a silo. Cross a road and at the next intersection turn left, then first right to pass the silo. Further on turn right onto a road and you come to Saint-Sauflieu.

SAINT-SAUFLIEU
♈ ♒ ▭
(see map ref 9)
Detour *1 hr 15 mins*
LOEUILLY
◠ ▲ ▭

Detour see left. Take a gravelled path heading south-west going through a wood, the Bois de Porte Nouvelle. Go past the locality known as Les Huit Journeaux, cross the D210 and walk down into the village of Loeuilly.

Cross the N16, follow the Rue des Seux and further on turn left into the Rue du Porissot until you come to an avenue bordered with lime trees. Pass the Rue du Bois on the right and carry on out of the village. Pass the wayside cross and turn right along the Chaussée Brunehaut. Carry straight on along the tarmac path running beside mixed woodland. Head towards the TV relay station. The GR meets a road near the village of Hébécourt, but does not go into the village. Turn left and leave the road at a bend, turning right at the memorial along a gravel path. Pass twice under the power line and when you come to a house standing alone take a gravel path to the left. At the second intersection (spot height 53) turn right along the edge of some woods. You come out on the D210 (spot height 45). Take the second path on the right leading to Dury.

10Km
2:30

DURY
✗ ♈ ♒ ▭
19th-century château, restored after the last war; commemorative plaque to Marshal Foch, who set up his headquarters here in 1918.

4Km
1:00

As you come into Dury there is a wayside cross. Turn left here along the Rue de l'Enfer, then left again towards Saleux. At the sign marking the edge of the village, take a dirt track on the right heading north-west. Pass two intersections, with the D210 and the D8, cross a little bridge over the River Selle, where on the right you will see two old water mills. Go along the Rue des Moutiers and you come to Salouël.

SALOUËL
✗ ♈ ♒ ▭
(see map ref 10)

At the lights in Salouël, the GR crosses the N29, turns left along it for 50 metres and then turns right into the Rue Jules-Verne. Take the

The Abbeys of the Somme

Our knowledge about the origins of Christianity in Picardy comes from tales which are for the most part based on precious little hard historical fact, but which do clearly reveal a tradition going back a long way.

One such tale is the story of St Firmin, who came from Spain and was martyred at Amiens at the end of the 3rd century; another is that of St Martin, since it was at Amiens in about 338 that, as a Roman soldier, he shared his cloak with a beggar.

The great invasions of the 5th century interrupted the line of bishops and their missionary work. With the towns collapsing all around them the remnants of the Empire regrouped around the first monasteries, many of them founded by Irish monks.

But it was during the Carolingian era that the monasteries had their golden age. Saint-Riquier and Corbie, with a close relative of the Emperor at their head, were unrivalled, bringing together all that mattered in the intellectual, artistic, religious and missionary life of the time. These monasteries also played an important part in the economy, giving rise to towns which eventually replaced the old Gallo-Roman ones.

From the middle of the 9th century the Norman invasion destroyed all these centres. Although Corbie found royal support in return for its loyalty, it is to the local lords and bishops that we owe the recovery of the monasteries and the founding of the many new ones during the 12th and 13th centuries.

The 100 Years War plunged the country into a period of serious unrest. Hostilities were renewed by the French king Francis I, against the forces of the Emperor and continued into the 17th century. Many monasteries decided to take permanent refuge inside the walled towns of the period, where many of them already had retreats. Monastery buildings were often occupied and destroyed, and the monks banished or accused of treason.

But abbey lands survived the ravages of war, and when peace came once more to the countryside the increase in farm rents meant that abbey revenues grew apace, allowing the monks to set about the task of rebuilding. But when the French Revolution abolished the abbeys, the monks were banished and the buildings and lands sold.

Yet anti-religious fury alone was not always responsible for the disappearance of these sanctuaries. Often abbeys fell into ruin because of prolonged neglect, a process hastened by thieves stripping the roofs of their lead. The remaining churches were taken over by the parishes. Buildings were converted to private dwellings when they were well situated, as at Saint-Valery, or turned into factories when the proximity of a stream or river provided motive power for the machinery, as at Séry. Others were reoccupied by religious communities. The law against congregations at the beginning of this century was another blow to the artistic heritage. Although the art treasures at Valloires just escaped dispersal, the buildings at Le Gard, on the other hand, were systematically plundered.

Life has now returned to several of the abbeys, among them Valloires, Saint-Riquier and Le Gard

PHILIPPE SEYDOUX
Abbeys of the Somme

3Km
0:45

PONT DE METZ
✕ ￥ ⚓ 🚌
Detour 1 hr 15 mins
AMIENS
🏠
Administrative centre of the
Somme and regional capital
of Picardy. See Walk 1, page
33.

2Km
0:30

SAVEUSE
⌂ 🚌

4Km
1:00

AILLY-SUR-SOMME
✕ ￥ ⚓ 🚐 🚌
(see map ref 11)

7Km
1:45

PICQUIGNY
🏠 ⛺ ✕ ￥ ⚓ 🚐
🚌
Collegiate church with 12th

path on the right, go under the railway bridge and turn right. After passing the games area turn left and climb towards Pont de Metz.

Detour see left. From the village of Pont de Metz, you can reach Amiens either along side roads via Renancourt and the Exhibition Centre, or by following the marked path shown as a detour (diverticule) by a broken line on the map.

Leaving Pont-de-Metz, the GR crosses the Rue du Château; then just before the church it turns right and runs along by the cemetery. Continue heading northwest, and at the intersection (spot height 69), just after passing under the power line, turn left. You pass close to a pumping station, then reach the D211. Follow this beside the wall of the château of Saveuse.

As you come into Saveuse the GR turns left along the Rue du Bois. At the junction carry straight on along the Rue d'Ailly. After passing a housing estate continue north, but before reaching Dreuil-les-Amiens, the GR bears left along a grassy path going under a power line. It meets a road along which you come to Ailly-sur-Somme.

As you come into Ailly-sur-Somme, the GR turns along the Rue D'Airaines towards the *collège*, and then across the D97, along the Rue Jules-Ferry. Continue along a path crossing fields and pastures. The path drops down into La Grande Vallée then climbs again into a wood, the Bois de l'Hermitage. Further on turn left along the D121 for 150 metres. After passing the Vallée des Vaux Jean turn to the right and head north along a tarred path. When you get to the top turn right along a path which takes you past the sports ground. Then do down the path to the left to Picquigny.

In Picquigny the GR turns right and when it reaches the presbytery turns left up the steps, L'Escalier Saint-Martin, leading to the church and the château. Pass through the grounds of

Picquigny

This town, defending one of the crossing places of the Somme, clings to the slopes of a valley overlooked by the ruins of the Château of the Vidames of Amiens. There is much to see there: gates with drawbridges, the house known as Le Pavillon de Sévigné, an enormous vaulted kitchen, and impressive walls along the hillside. There is also a fine view of the surrounding area.

The power and influence of the lords of Picquigny had much to do with their being the Vidames of Amiens, that is they were the secular arm of the bishop and were recorded as such as early as the eleventh century. By the end of the 13th century they owned three-quarters of the land around Amiens. They took part in all the great events of the Middle Ages, starting with the Norman conquest of England.

The treaty of 1475, bringing the 100 Years War to an official end, put Picquigny in the history books, but its role as a frontier town meant that it was frequently sacked and badly damaged during the 15th and 16th centuries. The old fortress passed through the hands of many owners until, finally, in the 19th century it gradually fell into a state of disrepair.

century Romanesque transept, high square tower (base 13th century, top 16th century), 13th century nave, 16th century apse; guided visits available on request. In the town square, old houses with stepped gables.

Detour *1 hr 30 mins*
ABBAYE DU GARD

The Cistercian Abbaye du Gard was founded in 1137. It is situated in pleasant green surroundings on the edge of extensive woodlands on a hillside sloping down to the Somme. The 18th century buildings are in the process of being restored by the assistant brothers of the clergy. The work on the big central building has largely been finished and the abbey has once more resumed its role as a centre for prayer and retreat. The route is shown by a broken line on the map.

1Km
0:15

the château and at the war memorial turn right down the steps leading to the town centre. Turn right, then left along the Rue du 60ᵉ, Régiment d'Infanterie. Turn left onto the N235, cross the railway line and the Canal de la Somme and you come to La Chaussée-Pirancourt.

LA CHAUSSÉE-TIRANCOURT
♟ 🚌

2Km
0:30

Gallic oppidum, archaeological reconstructions, visits.

Belloy-sur-Somme
(see map ref 12)

9Km
2:15

SAINT-OUEN
🏠 ✕ ♟ 🚏 🚌

10Km
2:30

L'ETOILE
🏠 ✕ ♟ 🚏 🚌

On the hillside overlooking the lakes on the right bank of the Somme, there is a Gallic oppidum, known as Caesar's camp, covering about 9.5 hectares, with a church dating to 1471. This area of the Somme valley is known for an unusual architectural feature, the Gothic-style tower, which was used until the 18th century: it is square, topped by an octagonally shaped stone spire, whose angles are decorated with leaf shapes and is found in the villages of Long, Fontaine, Cocquerel, Bourdon and Boucon.

4Km
1:00

As you come into the village turn right along the Rue de l'Abbreuvoir to come out in the square by the church. Carry straight on and then take the second turning on the left into the Rue de la Carrière until you reach Belloy-sur-Somme.

The GR leaves Belloy along a road heading north which crosses a bridge over the N1. You then cross the D81 and pass near a farm, the Ferme Saint-Accart. Further on the GR turns right onto a wide gravel path. Cross the D112 (spot height 64) and continue north-east and then north until you come to Saint-Ouen.

Entering St Ouen, the GR turns into the Rue Gambetta then left into the Rue de la Sence. Follow the road until you get to a farm, the Ferme du bois Riquier. About 500 metres further on, carry straight on along a grassy path bordered by a hedge. The GR then crosses the N1 (see map ref 13) and continues in a south-westerly direction. Beyond the wood, in the Vallée Delattre, turn right along a gravel path. When you come to the intersection of two dirt tracks turn left to face the village of Bouchon and its stone tower. The GR turns left onto the D216 and comes to L'Etoile.

The GR leaves the village of l'Etoile along the D112 in the direction of Long. At the wayside cross take the path to the right towards Bouchon. Almost immediately turn left onto a path crossing the Plaine D'Ailly. Cross the D10 and continue along an alley. At the first intersection, where there is a brick wayside cross, turn right, and then left into the Rue Joseph-Lévèque. Take a path on the left going down into the village of Long; turn right and walk down an alley in front of the church.

LONG

The church, partially reconstructed in the 19th century, retains a 16th century door and a tower with a carved stone spire of the same period. There is a two-storeyed 18th century château, in brick and stone, with a Mansart style roof; it is open to visitors from 20 August to 30 September. A traditional bonfire is held every year on St John's day, 23 June.

3Km
0:45

Detour *45 mins*
VILLERS-SOUS-AILLY

The route is marked by a broken line (Hors GR) on the map.

Detour *1 hr*
LONGPRÉ-LES-CORPS-SAINTS

The route is marked by a broken line (diverticule) on the map.

Cocquerel

(see map ref 14)
The church of Saint-Martin is one of the best examples in Picardy of a country church built in the local style. The low nave extends into an elegant 16th century chancel, the whole building being dominated by a 17th century tower topped by a stone steeple. In the nave there are some wood friezes; those in the chancel are of stone. The roof has huge remarkably carved beams.

3Km
0:45

FRANCIÈRES

The GR123 leaves Long along the D10 heading south. Over the bridge take the path to the right running beside the Somme. About 500 metres further on, at a bend in the river, take another path to the left going south-west which then crosses a bridge made of railway sleepers over a stream. After another 1.5 kilometres turn right and head north beside a pond; go over a concrete bridge and then turn right along a road until you come to Cocquerel.

As you come into Cocquerel the GR turns left along the D112. After the car park turn right onto a road heading north-west up to the higher ground. Then continue along a path towards the north-east. After passing a small wood on the left, leave this path and turn left along a road going down to Francières.

Leave the church behind you on the left and follow the road to the right. Just before you

4Km
1:00

reach the power line, turn right and, 100 metres further on, turn up a gravel path. At the top take a path on the left which passes under the power line and brings you to Ailly-Le-Haut-Clocher

AILLY-LE-HAUT-CLOCHER
✕ ♈ ♨ ▭

Situated at one of the highest points of the region, the church tower was used as an observation point in drawing the map of France. It was also used by the Germans as an observation post during the last war, until shells, aimed at the launching pads of the V1 and V2 rockets, damaged the 13th century building. The tower was rebuilt in 1957.

5Km
1:15

Leaving Ailly, the GR crosses the D10 and goes along a narrow alley to reach the N1. Cross this road and turn right along it for a few metres. Turn into the first alley on the left, pass by the *collège* and you come to Famechon. Turn left here and head north-west. Further on take the road on the left which passes the ruins of an old mill. After the cemetery, leave the road on the right and go down a path to the last houses of Bussus-Bussuel.

Bussus-Bussuel

5Km
1:15

The GR turns left along the D153. At the first bend leave the road on the left and continue straight on along a path passing a holiday camp. About 2.5 kilometres further on, bear right along the edge of a wood, go over the level crossing and turn left along the side of the railway. Then turn right into the Rue Notre-Dame until you come to the centre of Saint-Riquier.

SAINT-RIQUIER
🏠 ⌂ ✕ ♈ ♨ ▭
🛈

(see map ref 15)

5.5Km
1:20

In Saint-Riquier, after the sports ground, the GR turns left into the Rue du Nock. Turn left along the D925 and take the second alley on the right towards the picnic area. Continue along the path, which skirts a farm, the Ferme du Petit Moulin. At the first fork bear left along a path between two hedges. The GR crosses first a narrow road then the D82 and continues north-west until it comes to an intersection.

Intersection
(see map ref 16)
Detour *1 hr 45 mins*
ABBEVILLE
🏠 ✕ ♈ ♨ 🚌 ▭
The route is marked by a broken line (Hors GR) on the map.

Detour see left. At the intersection go straight on, heading west, pass to the south of the village of Drucat, climb to the top of the hill and follow a path south-west passing near a wood, the Bois des Catiches, which brings you to La Bouvaque. Go along the Rue du

Saint-Riquier

Formerly called Centule, the town owes its present name to a local monk, Riquier, who in the 7th century founded a monastery which King Dagobert showered with gifts. After Riquier's death, Centule Abbey, in which his remains were laid to rest, became a famous place of pilgrimage. Its prosperity grew still more during the reign of Charlemagne. Over the centuries, and as a consequence of the ravages of siege and fire, the town gradually declined as Abbeville, the estate of the abbot, grew in importance. A few ruins remain showing the outline of the abbey.

Destroyed twice and rebuilt again, the abbey-church is one of the finest medieval buildings in Picardy. Art lovers will find examples there of all periods of Gothic art, in particular:
● 12th century in the transept and chancel apse;
● flamboyant style from the end of the 15th century in the naves and the chapel overlooking the ambulatory.
In the 18th century, Abbot Charles d'Aligre added the classical touches of the panelling, screens and marble decoration.

The new abbey dates from the end of the 17th century. Since its acquisition by the Conseil Général de la Somme (Somme regional council) a cultural centre for the department has been established there, which puts on various exhibitions, concerts and lectures during the year. Guided visits of the abbey-church, free of charge, are given every day, except Mondays and Tuesdays. Other things to see:
In the town square: the belfry (12th--16th centuries); a house called La Maison de Napoléon, built by one of Napoleon's soldiers. The roof, shaped like his hat, is topped by a stone statuette of Napoleon I.

9Km
2:15

CANCHY

Scardon, then turn right to come to Place Victor-Hugo. Turn along the Chaussée du Bois and follow the main street through Abbeville until you reach the railway station.

At the intersection the GR takes the second path on the right and heads north above the village of Drucat to the left. Turn right onto the road to Millencourt. About 600 metres further on take the first path on the left. When you reach the crossroads where the D82 and D32 cross (spot height 53) turn left up the Fond du Moulin. Further on (spot height 72) take a tarmac path to the left and cross the D82 at Agenvillers sports ground. Bear right at the first fork and continue north-west in the same direction until you come to Canchy.

The GR passes in front of the church at Canchy, then passes the drive leading to the château. At the next intersection turn right and

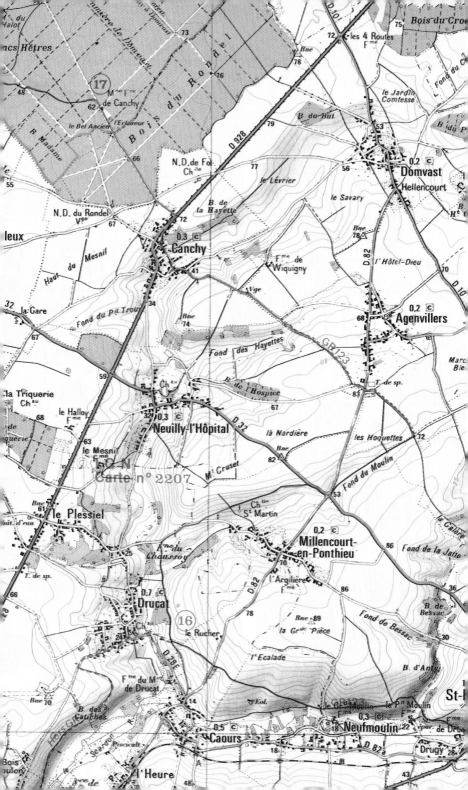

(see map ref 17)

5Km
1:15 **Maison Forestière de Canchy**

FOREST-L'ABBAYE
⌂ ✕ 🍷 🚌

7Km
1:45

you come to the D928. Turn right along this road out of the village. At this point turn left through a wood, the Bois du Rondel. Carry straight on into the Forêt Domaniale de Crécy. You then come to the Maison Forestière de Canchy.

The GR passes in front of the forester's house and 100 metres further on turns left along a path heading west. Cross a gravel path, walk through a clearing, keeping to the left, and further on take a path running along the edge of the forest until you get to the sports ground at Forest L'Abbaye.

Just north of Forest l'Abbaye the GR123 turns right and picks up the Chemin des Trois Mares, a path leading in a north-easterly direction. It crosses a wide forest road and continues towards a pond, the Mare du Hablot, which it skirts to the left. Further on (spot height 65) the GR bears left and follows a forest path north-east, which crosses three

The Forest of Crécy

Crécy State Forest, covering an area of 4,314 hectares, is the biggest area of forest in the Somme. It was once a dependency of the Comté de Ponthieu, and was held in pledge by the Duc de Guise in the middle of the 17th century. In Colbert's time it provided plenty of timber; coppicing provided firewood, and the trees left to grow to maturity were used in ship building.

There are various species of tree in the forest, notably beech and oak – of which several are extremely old and are listed as historical monuments –but also hornbeam and elm. Some reach massive proportions such as Le Chêne des Ramolleux, L'Hermite, and Le Hêtre de la Vierge, which has a girth of more than 4 metres.

The forest today is all that remains of the immense forest of Gaul, which once stretched from the Seine to the Scheldt. Impenetrable and full of wild life, it offered shelter and food to man, who soon colonised it. The existence of Gallic settlements is proved by the presence of numerous graves known as *tombelles*, and also by the places used for their religious ceremonies. It was held in respect by the Romans, who did no more than make roads through it; but large areas were later cleared by monks. It was the refuge of hermits seeking solitude and provided shelter for Riquier, who, after founding the Abbey of Centule (see page 103), came to end his days at the Hermitage. The counts of Pontheiu, the kings of England, the dukes of Burgundy, all came to this famous hunting ground and King Louis XI had a hunting lodge at La Haute Loge.

Boar are always present and sometimes very abundant in migratory years. Roe deer are on the increase.

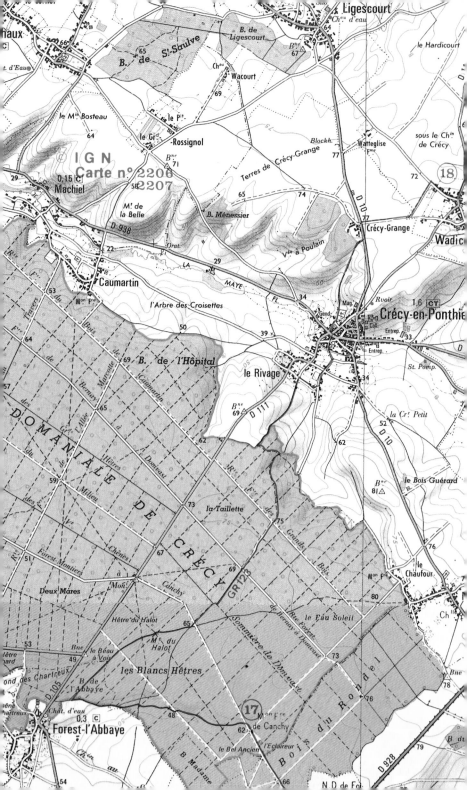

forest roads, the Canchy, Bernay and Grands-Bois. About 200 metres after the Grands-Bois road, it leaves the path and turns left onto an old railway line. Turn left, then right and continue down into Crécy-en-Ponthieu.

CRÉCY-EN-PONTHIEU

🏠 ✕ ☐ ☐ ☐ ☐

Besides a rather unusual monument dating from the end of the 12th century, Crécy has a 16th century church with a porch on the side in the flamboyant style. Also of interest: the Emhisarc municipal museum, Rue des Écoles (two rooms: geology and paleontology, prehistory).

3Km
0:45

The GR runs along by the Crécy-en-Ponthieu cemetery. At Crécy-Grange cross the D10 and from there continue to Wadicourt.

Wadicourt

(see map ref 18)
19th century church.

5Km
1:15

After passing the cemetery at Wadicourt the GR bears right along a path (north-east). Cross the Chaussée Brunehaut and drop down the Fond du Val. At Voisin turn left along the road. Continue to Dompierre-sur-Authie.

The Battle of Crécy

At Crécy-en-Ponthieu on 26 August 1346 this famous battle in the 100 Years' War ended in a crushing defeat for the French. King Edward III with a fleet of 1,100 vessels had set sail to go to the aid of his Duchy of Guyenne, threatened by the eldest son of Philippe VI of Valois. The vagaries of the wind forced him to land on the peninsula of Cotentin in Normandy, and after venturing with his army as far as the outskirts of Paris, he thought it prudent to withdraw to the Comté de Ponthieu, one of his possessions. The French king pursuing Edward with an army of 100,000 men arrived from Marcheville and just after midday encountered the English army drawn up in position on a hillside to the north overlooking the village. The French attacked from the low ground, Genoese crossbowmen out front. But a rainstorm had soaked the bowstrings, severely reducing their firing power, and so the Genoese scattered. Suspecting some sort of treachery, the knights of the Comte d'Alençon charged them. In the confusion which ensued the poor devils retaliated by slicing the horses' hamstrings. In fury the horsemen then made charge after charge, but the English, sheltering behind their waggons, put up a very effective defence. Night brought a halt to the carnage: on the battlefield, on the French side, the King of Bohemia, Jean de Luxembourg, 1,200 horsemen and 30,000 infantrymen lay dead.

At the site of the battle a monument was erected in memory of the old, blind King of Bohemia, who perished there.

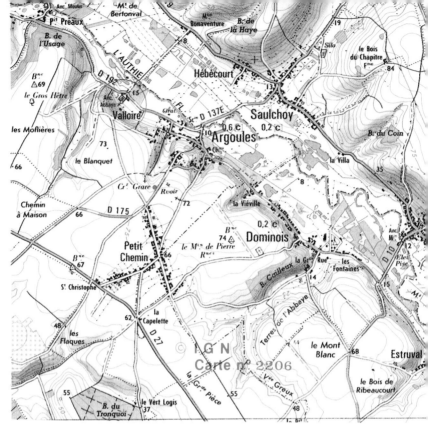

DOMPIERRE-SUR-AUTHIE

🍷 ⚒ 🚌

*The town used to have a
castle belonging to the
Chatillons, where Louis XI
stayed in 1464. Today it
consists merely of a 16th
century tower and a tall
construction built in 1627 of
stone and brick. There is a
15th century church.*

Detour *2 hrs 15 mins*

Abbaye de Valloires

*Nothing remains of the
abbey founded in 1143 by
the Cistercians, but the
buildings reconstructed in
the 18th century have a unity
of style seldom seen and a
quite classical elegance.
They contain some
exceptional panelling by
Pfaffenhofen in different*

5Km
1:15

At Dompierre-sur-Authie the GR turns right
along the D111 and heads north-east. About 1
kilometre further on leave this road and climb
left to a wood, the Bois de Rue. Carry on and
then drop down into a ravine, the Ravin de la
Goulaffre. At this point turn right along the road
and then take a path on the left leading to
Mouriez.

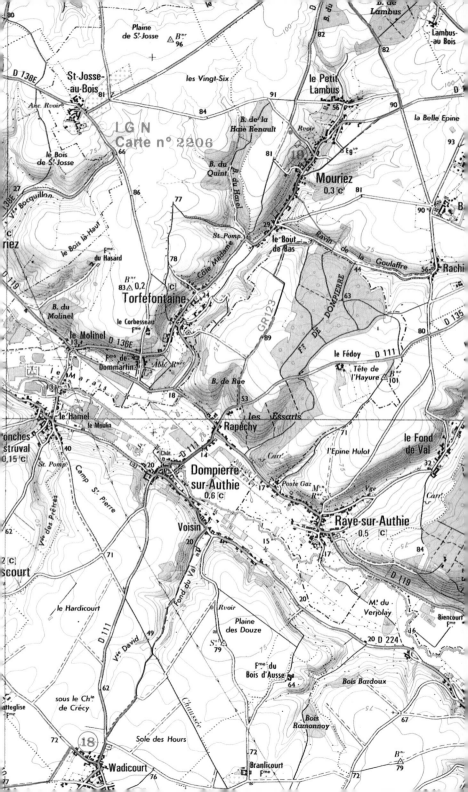

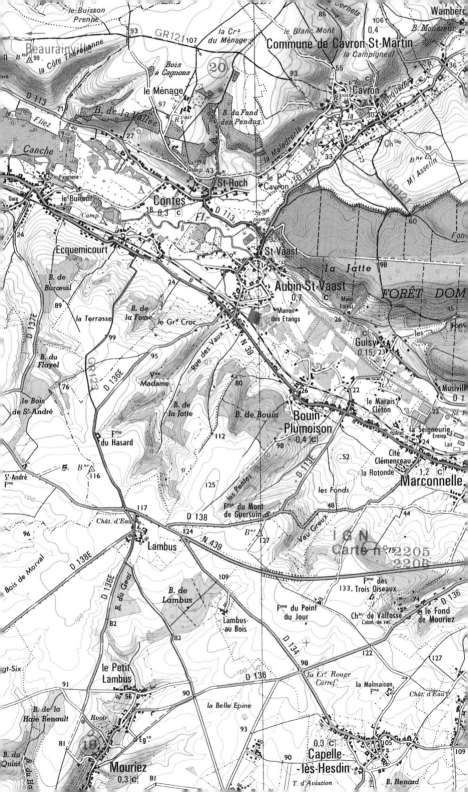

apartments and in the chapel, the former abbey-church, where there are also some admirable screens by Jean Veyren and the recumbent statues of Marie de Ponthieu and Simon de Dammartin (13th century).

Mouriez
(see map ref 19)

10Km
2:30

At Mouriez the GR heads up to the church via a path on the right. Turn right beyond the church onto the D136. At the first crossroads (spot height 90) turn left and head for Lambus. There the GR takes the D135E heading north-west. After passing a farm, the Ferme du Hasard, leave the road and follow a path on the left leading to Ecquemicourt. Turn right along the N39, then take the first left to cross the railway line. Head right alongside the railway line and when you get to the church turn left and skirt the cemetery of Aubin-St-Vaast.

AUBIN-SAINT-VAAST

4Km
1:00

Take the D154 until you come to Saint-Vaast, then the D113 to the left towards Contes (café). Turn right here, pass through St-Roch, a wayside cross, and go up through a valley, the Bois du Fond des Pendus. At the top of the hill you come to a place where the paths cross, marking the junction with the GR121.

Junction with the GR121
(see map ref 20)

4Km
1:00

Taking the GR121 to the left brings you to Beaurainville; to the right it brings you to Hesdin.

BEAURAINVILLE

9Km
2:15

HESDIN

See Walk 2, page 51.

WALK 4

The GR127 starts from the hamlet of Louez-les-Duisans, in the commune district of Duisans, 6 kilometres north-west of the town of Arras. The start of the footpath can be reached by rail or bus via Arras, or by rail via Duisans Halt.

ARRAS

🏛 ⌂ ⚑ ✕ ♟ ⚖
🚌 🚃

Arras, Préfecture for the Pas-de-Calais region, has interesting architecture with squares in the Flemish style, Hôtel de Ville and bell-tower of 14th to 18th centuries; 18th century Saint-Vaast abbey; museum.

From Arras railway station:

● head north-west across the town towards Lens as far as Saint-Catherine's church, where you will find the western section of the GR121. Follow this via the D341, across the River Scarpe, past a fish farm and a factory (6 kilometres, 1 hour 35 minutes walking);

● or catch a bus as far as Saint-Catherine's church and continue along the GR121 towards Louez (4 kilometres, 1 hour);

● or get a bus from Arras to the mayor's office (mairie) at Anzin-Saint Aubin, and pick up the GR121 at Anzin mill (3 kilometres, 45 minutes);

● or else catch the town bus for the Résidence Saint-Pol. On reaching the terminus pick up the GR121 some 400 metres north-west along a cart track. Louez-les-Duisans is 2.2 kilometres and 35 minutes away.

From Duisans railway halt:
head northeast along the D55, cross the N39 and continue along a tarred path still heading north-east towards a factory clearly visible in the distance to reach Louez-les-Duisans 1.5 kilometres and 20 minutes away.

LOUEZ-LES-DUISANS
✕

1.7Km
0:20

From Louez-les-Duisans the GR127 follows the D60 northwards, crosses the River Scarpe by an old mill lock, goes left along the D60E, and 200 metres farther on continues left along a riverside path for anglers. It then crosses a marshy area planted with poplars, bears right as it draws level with a culvert, and on coming to an outfall turns left along a tarmac path past the Sainte Bertille Spring.

Sainte-Bertille Spring

Legend has it that this spring, said to cure eye conditions, came forth at the

0.7Km
0:10
saint's bidding in the 8th

The path leads on to the little township of Maroeuil.

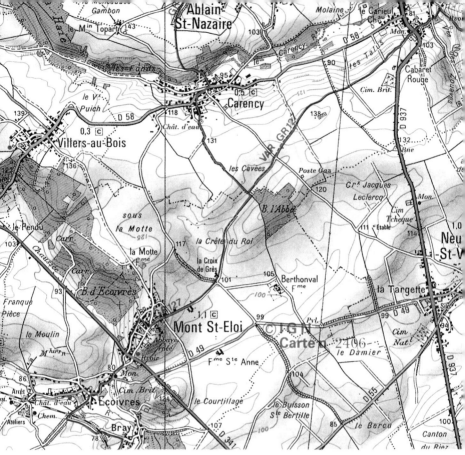

century. A site of pilgrimage
on the Sunday nearest 8
October.

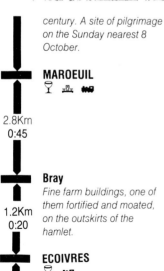

MAROEUIL
♀ ⛴ 🍺

2.8Km
0:45

Bray
*Fine farm buildings, one of
them fortified and moated,
on the outskirts of the
hamlet.*

1.2Km
0:20

ECOIVRES
♀ 🍺
Baronial farm, château and

Go left along the D56, cross the Scarpe and
then the railway track to the left of the station,
and take a path to the right which is tarred at
first, then gravelled. It follows the line of the
railway track for 1,500 metres, crosses it, and
continues on a tarmac path to the hamlet of
Bray.

Turn left on to a tarred road which runs along
above the the railway, with a view of Mont-Eloi
to join a narrow local road, where you turn right
under the railway bridge, cross the Scarpe
again and reach the hamlet of Ecoivres.

Continue along the D49 to the right. Notice the
spring on the left. After 500 metres take a
narrow tarred road to the left of the wayside

1.3Km
0:25

church. Some 700 metres to the north are the so-called 'standing stones' or 'devil's stones' or 'twin stones', the origin of which is disputed.

Calvary, which climbs towards the ruins of Mont-Saint-Eloi abbey. After another 300 metres, opposite and below an enclosing wall, follow a footpath to the left, which widens to an alley before reaching the D341. Cross this road and go up the village street for 300 metres, turning right on to a footpath skirting some gardens, then left to the great open square in front of the ruins of Mont-Saint-Eloi abbey.

MONT-SAINT-ELOI ABBEY

135m

Views over Lower Artois and Arras. Remains of fortified medieval abbey. Ruins of 18th century abbey church rased during the Revolution except for the towers, which were damaged by military action in 1915.

4.5Km
1:05

To leave the hill on which the abbey stands, first skirt around the abbey precinct, heading north-east, then keep straight on until you reach a sharp right-hand bend on a gently rising tarmac track, which degenerates into an earth path, and soon becomes sunken and overgrown. At the Abbey Wood (Bois l'Abbé) turn left along a grassy, earth path which heads north-west and widens into a forestry service road, with views over the valleys of Carency and La Souchez, Lorette hill and Liévin mining basin. This track leads to Carency.

CARENCY

2Km
0:30

The GR127 crosses the D58 and a little farther on takes a minor local road on the left. This crosses Carency stream, then climbs quickly up the opposite slope. After 300 metres it takes a dirt path on the right which eventually

Abbey de Mont St Eloi

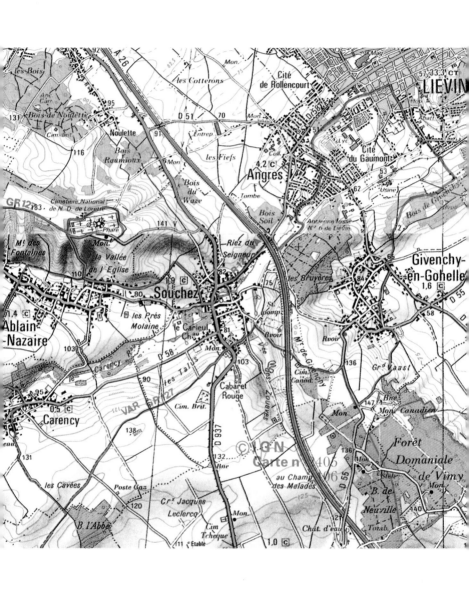

becomes tarmac, drops down again, rejoins the tarred minor road and crosses the D57 to Ablain-Saint-Nazaire.

ABLAIN-SAINT-NAZAIRE
♟ ⚓

Large village along a main street; rebuilt after the 1914–18 war. Remains of 15th–16th century church situated one kilometre to the east.

1.7Km
0:25

The street continues as a grass footpath. This brings you to a footbridge across Saint-Nazaire stream, at the foot of the imposing hill, Notre-Dame de Lorette. Take the footpath on the right. After 400 metres the footpath joins a country path. Keep straight on in an easterly direction. Pass a playing field and bear left. Beyond a short gully take a tarred minor road known locally as the 'voie blanche', or white way. This road goes up to the Notre-Dame de Lorette memorial. Taking the lantern tower as a landmark, leave this minor road in another 150 metres and take a pathway which becomes increasingly overgrown and eventually comes out on the Lorette plateau.

NOTRE-DAME DE LORETTE NATIONAL CEMETERY
♟

Shelter for visitors 500 metres north of the memorial; Chapel at an elevation of 175 metres; Extensive views: to the north east the mining basin and Flandres plain, to the east the Vimy ridge with its own memorial, to the south the vale of Saint-Nazaire, the

3.5Km
0:50

plateaux of Lower Artois and the bluff of Mont Saint-Eloi. The National Cemetery contains 18,000 graves from the 1914–18 war. The lantern tower, 52 metres high, visitors admitted, stands on top of a mausoleum holding 16,000 unidentified fallen.

From the war memorial, the GR heads westwards to the left, along the tarred path leading to the visitors' centre. It then turns left at the western end of the cemetery along a wide, flat cart track. This is gravelled to begin with, but after passing some kennels it shows increasing signs of damage from forestry vehicles. This track continues along the ridge of the Lorette plateau, giving some lovely views over Ablain. It goes into the forest (oak, beech, ash and even a few chestnut trees despite the latitude). A muddy stretch leads to an intersection. Turn right here and then keep straight ahead at another crossroads 50 metres farther on. Proceed north-eastwards along a forest trail which is hard to make out in places and flanked with the boundary hedges of private properties. **Warning** keep to the waymarked trail and take great care in the hunting season. The waymarking is unclear, having been damaged by hunters. After another 300 metres, at spot height 187 metres, the GR bears a little to the left and follows a flat forest ride – note the many chestnut trees. Some 500 metres farther on, at a crossroads, the GR turns right down a slippery path and then takes the left-hand fork 200 metres from there. It continues along the forest edge, then turns down to the right, towards the allotments in the mining village of Marqueffles.

Marqueffles

Here you can still see signs of No 1 Pit at the Gouy-Servins mine, and the abrupt escarpment of the fault line marking the boundary between Artois and the Plain of Flandres, topped by the Lorette war memorial.

1.8Km
0:25

Opposite a hospice, turn left and join a path on the left leading south west towards the escarpment. At the edge of the forest turn right on to a rutted cart track which skirts the base of the escarpment. Go ahead at the crossroads and this brings you to Bouvigny-Boyeffles.

BOUVIGNY-BOYEFFLES
♟ ⚓

2.7Km
0:40

Cross the first street you come to, and at the second you will find, just a few paces to the left, a straight, narrow pathway with barbed wire alongside. This crosses the grounds of a former château, now a private institution, and after 500 metres you come to the D75 road. **Warning** Going in the reverse direction, the start of this pathway is behind a hedge and difficult to spot from the D75. Turn right and after 150 metres turn left on to a track which is macadamized at first, then gravelled, and eventually only dirt. It brings you to some crossroads at 118 metres.

Detour *30 mins*
HERAIN-COUPIGNY
♟ ⚓ ▭

Detour see left. Turn right at the 118 metres marker and find 'Estate No 10'. Reach the centre from there along the D188 road, 2 kilometres in all.

At the crossroads the GR footpath goes left up a steep earth path to the artesian plateau at 188 metres, near the Bouvigny television relay tower.

Bouvigny television relay tower

Tower built in 1963, at that time the tallest of its kind in Europe. Visible from over 25 kilometres away, it makes an invaluable landmark for walkers.

2.3Km
0:35

At the 188 metres marker the footpath goes to the right along a gravelled track, and then right again another 500 metres along a grass path where waymarking is unclear. It crosses the D65 and skirts the much thinned Verdrel woods. At the western edge of the wood, which is not easy to spot, it turns left along a narrow earth track through grazing land and brings you to the hamlet of Verdrel.

VERDREL
♟ ⚓

A narrow alley with walls on either side brings you to the D57E. Follow this road left and go through the entire village. Beyond a housing estate you come to the southern end of Olhain woods, mainly state forest. At a wayside cross turn right on to a forestry service track.

Detour *10 mins*
Fresnicourt dolmen
*Sole remnant of a much
larger group of megaliths.
Go south along the D57E
road for about 600 metres
and turn left.*

**4.7Km
1:10**

After another 600 metres the forestry track
reaches the western edge of the woods, which
the GR follows, along a clearly defined path
heading north west. From here you can
overlook a low-lying area known in geological
terms as the 'Weald', known locally as 'Bray',
of Houdain. The GR cuts through the woods
for 200 metres on a poorly defined path, and
then drops down to a parking area beside the
D57E. It crosses this road and continues up a
steep path which comes once more to the
western edge of the wood. The route then
drops down steeply to a place called the
'sheep fold', until recently a heath with rare
plant species on a superb south-facing ex-
posure, but now turned into a golf course. Skirt
around the north of this area, keeping to the
edge of the wood, and join a good gravelled
track which drops down to Olhain. **Warning**
Walking in the reverse direction, the route
round the golf course is not obvious.

OLHAIN
⛺ ✗ 🍷
*Medieval castle of 13th–16th
centuries, surrounded by a
lake, open on Sundays and
public holidays.*
Detour *15 mins*
**OLHAIN DEPARTMENTAL
LEISURE CENTRE**
⛺ 🍷 🚌

**1.5Km
0:20**
*Sports facilities. Swimming
pool.*

Detour, see left. Beyond the golf course,
follow the gravel track to the right for 1
kilometre.

From the castle, the GR footpath follows the
D57 road to the right, passes an intersection
with a cross made from a single block of
sandstone, and after 200 metres turns to the
right along a tarred track which brings you to
Gauchin-Légal.

GAUCHIN-LÉ GAL
or Gauchin-le-Gal
✗ 🍷 🚌
*In the market square notice
the 'Gal', a round block of
sandstone fixed to a
boundary marker. Get*

**2Km
0:30**

Cross the D341 – old Roman road – and
continue left along the D73 from the church to
the cemetery, where the GR takes a path to the
right. This is tarred at first, but unsurfaced
farther on. It comes out to the right on to a
gravelled track which goes down to Hermin.

someone to tell you the story behind it.

Hermin

1.8Km
0.25

From the church continue up the gently sloping D72 to the water tower, and take a dirt track on the right which has all but disappeared. This slopes gently down to rejoin the D72. At a crossroads with the D341, the GR footpath takes a minor road to the left, which follows the line of the old Roman road from Arras to Boulogne. **Warning** waymarking unclear – take particular care going in the reverse direction. At the bottom of the next dip are a few houses on the outskirts of Rebreuve-sous-les-Monts.

REBREUVE-SOUS-LES-MONTS

2.5Km
0:35

Village centre, 500 metres to the north, on the D341 road:

The GR footpath continues north west along the line of the Roman road for 800 metres. At the second crossroads, near Ranchicourt village, it heads left along a track which is tarred at first and then gravelled, climbing gently up the southern slope of the Bray of Houdain.

Detour
HOUDAIN

Church of 12th–16th centuries; feudal motte.

4.7Km
1:10

Detour see left. From the crossroads near Ranchicourt, keep along the Roman road for 1.5 kilometres and turn right towards the town centre.

At the top of the plateau the GR becomes grassy and takes the first path on the left, where waymarking is unclear, with a view over the western part of the mining basin, the Bruay and Auchel spoil tips. After 500 metres the GR continues to the right along a tarmac path which goes down towards a thicket, past some farms, across the D86 and into La Comté.

LA COMTÉ

The GR crosses the river Lawe near an old mill, passes a farm/château, comes to the church and keeps straight on towards the south west up a gently sloping grass path. It then intersects with a tarred minor road and climbs towards the Ternois plateau, passing through a heavily overgrown sunken section some 300 metres long. A sunken water supply installation stands at a tricky intersection at 140 metres, where you turn at an angle to the right along the least obvious path, ignoring the good, straight path.

6.8Km
1:40

The GR footpath heads north west and then north across some flattish countryside. Way-marking is not possible along here. Go through the fields across a 100-metre gap. The GR then makes a right-left dog-leg across a minor road and keeps going due north along a path which gradually peters out, with another gap. It then bears north west along a cutting on the disused railway from Saint-Pol to Houdain. A clearly marked path crosses the cutting, heads north again, comes to a hedge and brings you to the tarred minor road from Bajus to Diéval; where you turn left.

Warning In reverse direction this is a tricky stretch, with limited waymarking. Leave the minor road at the sharp left-hand bend and take the path on the left.

The GR footpath then drops down to Diéval.

DIÉVAL

Turn right at the next crossroads to a small chapel. From there go down a steep gravelly path to the N41 road. The GR turns left up the N41 for 100 metres before turning right into a street which comes out below the church. The footpath route goes up the steps and across the churchyard, passes the porch and meets the gently climbing D89 road on the left. At the next crossroads it turns right and then left along a wide country road which is tarmac at first, then gravel, and finally runs through grass, heading north west alongside the La Lihue woods.

4.7Km
1:10

Beyond two more crossroads the GR comes to a tarmac road overlooking the Val de Clarence. It heads left, south west, continuing as an unsurfaced track which goes through a small wood, then narrows down past an enclosure till it comes to the viewing point on Les Equer-guettes hill, overlooking Bours village and its château. A very steep descent across lime-stone heath brings you to a country path which turns to the right through the tunnel under the railway, to reach Bours.

BOURS

Feudal keep, some 350

Some 100 metres beyond the tunnel, the GR turns right, due north, along a track which is tarred at first. Keep straight on as you draw

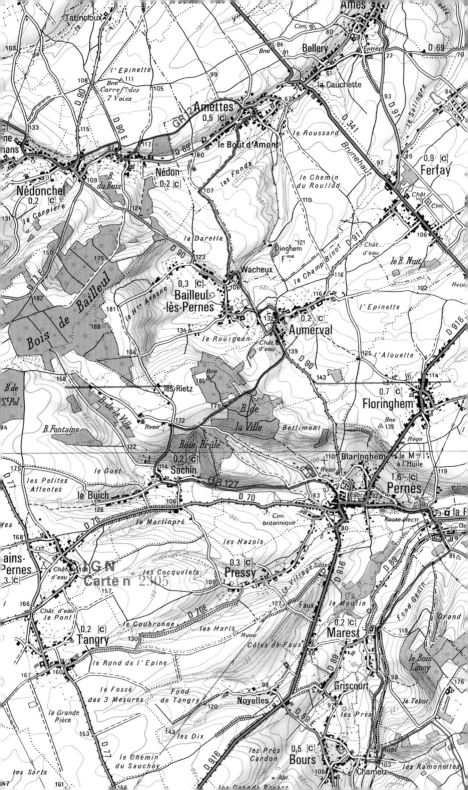

metres off the footpath.

3.8Km
0.55

LA FERTÉ
Pernes-Camblain station

2Km
0:30

PERNES-EN-ARTOIS

2.2Km
0:35

Sachin-les-Pernes

level with a straight service road, heading across the fields. The GR picks up the line of a footpath some 20 metres farther on and is once more easy to trace. It bears right at the top of a rise and makes for the railway line, going under the railway at the first intersection, along several metres of tarmac, and turning left immediately beyond the tunnel along an unsurfaced track close beside the track-bed.

After a few more metres, the GR turns left on to a wide gravelled track as far as the level-crossing at Marest, where it turns right on to an almost flat gravelled track heading north west. There is an overgrown section some 150 metres long before you reach the tarred local road leading to the cement factory and railway station at La Ferté.

The GR footpath continues along the D70 road to Pernes, crosses the Clarence near an old mill, skirts a quarry for Palaeozoic sandstone and schist, then turns right along a track and immediately left. The gravel section of this path crosses some gardens. A tarred stretch then intersects the D916 and follows the Rue du Bart as far as the church at Pernes-en-Artois, where it goes round to the left and brings you to the front of the building.

Warning In the reverse direction the way-marking for turning right into the Rue du Bart is unclear.

Some 500 metres beyond the church, the GR turns left along a footpath with hedges on either side and brings you to an intersection. There it takes the second path on the right, which is gravelled, and climbs gently, then in another 300 metres continues left on an unsurfaced path along the Clarence valley to Sachin-les-Pernes.

Turning right towards the church, the footpath continues along a narrow road which climbs sharply to the 'Mont Rôti' and turns right at the top before continuing left 300 metres farther on along a gravelled track which climbs to the communal woodland Bois de la Ville. On reaching the woods, keep heading northeast

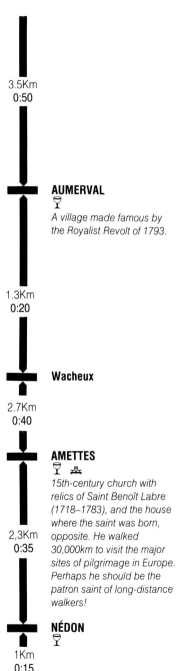

3.5Km
0:50

AUMERVAL
A village made famous by
the Royalist Revolt of 1793.

1.3Km
0:20

Wacheux

2.7Km
0:40

AMETTES
15th-century church with
relics of Saint Benoît Labre
(1718–1783), and the house
where the saint was born,
opposite. He walked
30,000km to visit the major
sites of pilgrimage in Europe.
Perhaps he should be the
patron saint of long-distance
walkers!

2,3Km
0:35

NÉDON

1Km
0:15

in the same direction as the path, which suddenly narrows down to a little trail before dropping down through a rather overgrown tunnel of overhanging boughs, where way-marking is unclear. This brings you to a gravelled track after another 300 metres.

Warning From the reverse direction: this section is tricky and hard to spot. Do not stray on to the grazing land.

On reaching the D90 road turn left to Aumerval.

At the water tower the GR footpath turns right, then left at the church, and continues along a paved track flanked with hedges. After 300 metres, at a sharp right-hand bend, look to your left for a trail crossing the fields, where waymarking is unclear, all that remains of a country path heading west–south-west. The route eventually becomes more obvious and joins a gravelled track, where it turns right. In another 400 metres there is a view over the village of Bailleul-les-Pernes and its church. The GR drops down into the hamlet of Wacheux.

The route continues up the hollow along a rather wet, sunken path, and joins a tarred path on the right. Farther on it becomes gravel, then after a kilometre turns right on to another gravelled track, and drops down to Amettes.

The footpath comes out opposite the saint's house, turns left along the D69 road for 50 metres, then right and left again up a steep street between walls. At a right-hand bend, the GR route takes an unsurfaced path on the left heading southwest. This climbs gently up to the hilltops overlooking the river Nave, cuts across another path, skirts a wood and joins a wide, gravelled track which goes left down to Nédon.

At the bottom of the slope, a footpath on the right goes straight to the church. The GR goes to the right up a tarred road for 200 metres and turns left on to an unsurfaced path which

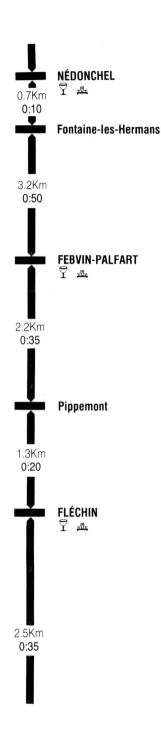

NÉDONCHEL

0.7Km
0:10

Fontaine-les-Hermans

3.2Km
0:50

FEBVIN-PALFART

2.2Km
0:35

Pippemont

1.3Km
0:20

FLÉCHIN

2.5Km
0:35

comes to the farms of Nédonchel.

The GR goes left down the D90 road, then turns right along the D69 as it follows the river Nave to Fontaine-les-Hermans.

The GR then goes to the right up a tarred minor road, and after 300 metres turns left on to a long tarmac path, which runs at the foot of the escarpment along the Artois fault line. On reaching a crossroads with the D94, the GR turns left along the road for some 400 metres before turning right on to a gravelled track which joins the D95 on the outskirts of Febvin-Palfart.

From the church, the GR footpath continues to the right along the D77 for 300 metres, then turns right on to a gravelled track. After another 300 metres it turns off to the left along a muddy track passing close to a farm with a château. There it crosses another path and follows the Puits sans fond stream heading north west. The path climbs a little, takes on a tarmac surface and joins a minor road leading to Pippemont.

Some 100 metres before the chapel in this hamlet, the GR turns left down an overgrown path alongside the stream and then crosses over. It turns right along an earth track on the other bank which eventually acquires a gravelled surface, and rejoins the D77 outside Fléchin.

From the tiny square, go to the right along a narrow street to the church. Continue along an unsurfaced track beside a stream and bear right along a very narrow section – only 70 centimetres wide – between two barbed wire fences with a view of a medieval motte. The footpath then crosses the Puits sans fond stream by a lightly-built footbridge, comes to a tarred minor road, crosses it and follows a path rising abruptly north-eastwards. At the top, turn left along a tarred track which rejoins the minor road on the edge of a wood. Turn left and then immediately right along an earth path which crosses a neck of the woods and then heads north west along the edge of the trees.

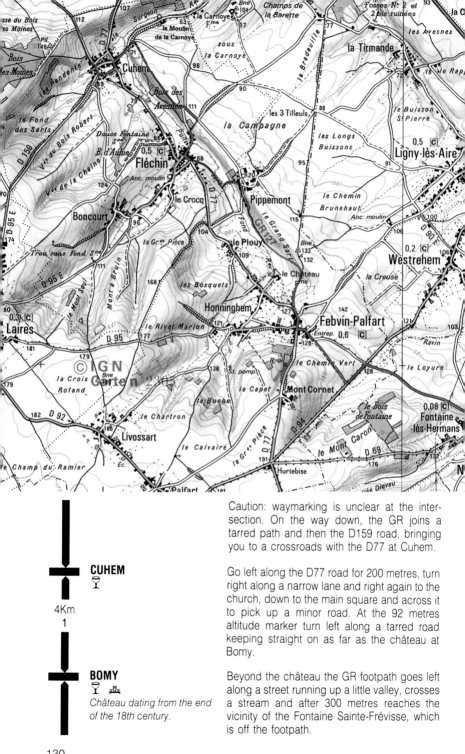

CUHEM
♊

4Km
1

BOMY
♊ ⚓

*Château dating from the end
of the 18th century.*

Caution: waymarking is unclear at the intersection. On the way down, the GR joins a tarred path and then the D159 road, bringing you to a crossroads with the D77 at Cuhem.

Go left along the D77 road for 200 metres, turn right along a narrow lane and right again to the church, down to the main square and across it to pick up a minor road. At the 92 metres altitude marker turn left along a tarred road keeping straight on as far as the château at Bomy.

Beyond the château the GR footpath goes left along a street running up a little valley, crosses a stream and after 300 metres reaches the vicinity of the Fontaine Sainte-Frévisse, which is off the footpath.

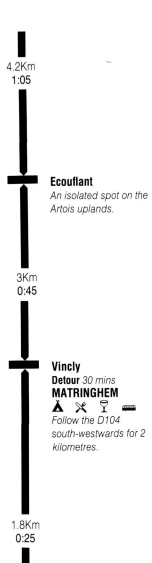

4.2Km
1:05

Ecouflant
*An isolated spot on the
Artois uplands.*

3Km
0:45

Vincly
Detour *30 mins*
MATRINGHEM
*Follow the D104
south-westwards for 2
kilometres.*

1.8Km
0:25

The GR does not cross the culvert, but turns right on to a tarmac path with hedges on either side. This comes out to the D130, where you turn left for 50 metres and then take the right-hand fork along a gently climbing track which at first is tarred, then gravelled, and finally unsurfaced. As you head south west, ignore several crossings and side turnings, and after 2.5 kilometres you come to the D92 road. Turn right along it to the hamlet of Ecouflant.

By the ruined chapel turn left off the D92 on to a tarmac path going south westwards for 700 metres, then turn right on to a gravel track, with extensive views of the Lys valley. After another 700 metres go left down a narrow unsurfaced trail, which widens, acquires a tarmac surface, and continues along a cultivated valley bottom until it meets a tarred path. Turn right along this into Vincly.

Warning The waymarking on this stretch is unclear, particularly when followed in the reverse direction.

The GR footpath crosses the D104, goes down a tarred track in the direction of the river Lys, and comes to a gate on to some marshy common land. Here you have a choice of routes. One way is to cross the marsh, heading straight for a metal footbridge over the Lys 300 metres away; but there are some very muddy and even dangerous stretches where you could sink in. The other possibility is to follow the waymarking along the tarred track to the right of the gate as far as a house. The track continues over grass for 20 metres to a barbed wired gate. Go through, remembering to shut it behind you, and down a short slope to the foot of the valley. You can now see the footbridge.

Warning This is a difficult section in the reverse direction. On the other side of the Lys, the GR footpath bears right and joins the bed of an old branch railway line running along the bottom of the valley. The path is open in some places and overgrown in others. It continues along a dirt road serving local quarries, which tends to be muddy, and brings you to Bellefontaine.

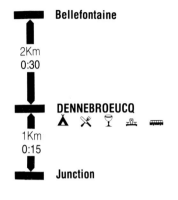

Bellefontaine

DENNEBROEUCQ

Junction

2Km
0:30

1Km
0:15

The old railway station is easy to spot on the right. The route again joins the bed of this old line from Fruges to Aire-sur-la-Lys, where the going is now good, and continues among some residential caravans. Turn right on to the busy D157 road to Dennebroeucq.

On entering the village the GR footpath turns left, due west along a track which is tarred at first, then gravelled, leading to a crossing of the ways.

At the crossways the GR127A, the Southern Branch and the GR127B, the Northern Branch, separate.

GR127A; DENNEBROEUCQ–DALLES

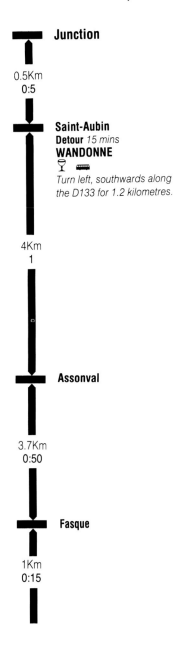

Junction

0.5Km
0:5

Saint-Aubin
Detour *15 mins*
WANDONNE
🍷 🚌

*Turn left, southwards along
the D133 for 1.2 kilometres.*

4Km
1

Assonval

3.7Km
0:50

Fasque

1Km
0:15

From the junction where the southern and northern branches, the GR127A and 127B, separate, keep straight on along the gravelled track in a westerly direction. The GR127A crosses the D133 near the Saint-Aubin farm/château.

The GR127A keeps heading due west along an unsurfaced path. After 300 metres this crosses another, wider path.

The GR, now partly gravelled, climbs steadily towards the Bois-Vieille ridge – 183 metres. On the tops, near a derelict farm, the footpath crosses an earth track and after 100 metres bears left, at another crossways.

Caution, especially when coming in the reverse direction, as waymarking is tricky in this section. The GR then crosses the D928 road and bends southwest. It takes a left-hand fork after 250 metres – waymarking unclear, crosses another dirt path some 500 metres farther on, and then drops quickly down through a muddy section towards Assonval.

The GR crosses a square and turns left up the D129E for 300 metres. It then turns right, along a gravelled track which soon becomes grassy heading southwest. After another kilometre it takes a right-hand fork on to a narrow dirt track alongside the hedges of Gournay hamlet. It crosses another dirt path and then meets a surfaced track, which it follows to the right, north-westwards, down to the hamlet of Fasque.

On reaching the first buildings, the GR turns sharp left down a track to a lower level, then after 50 metres turns right into a sunken lane which crosses the D129 and continues as a tarred pathway on the flat. Some 200 metres farther on it turns left along a tarred track which then turns to gravel, muddy in places, with hedges on either side, following the

135

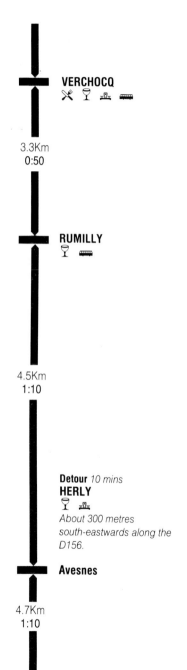

VERCHOCQ

3.3Km
0:50

RUMILLY

4.5Km
1:10

Detour *10 mins*
HERLY
*About 300 metres
south-eastwards along the
D156.*

Avesnes

4.7Km
1:10

alluvial valley of the Aa. The route crosses a street and rejoins the D129 road near the church at Verchocq.

The GR127A then follows the D148 road towards Rumilly for 200 metres and draws level with the park of an 18th-century château, where it takes a tarred track to the right, crosses the Aa, and continues up a gravelled track through a combe, alongside a little wood. At the top the GR turns left along another gravel track, where the waymarking is unclear, then runs down to a farm with views over the Aa valley, and continues on a tarred track, reaching the bottom of the valley at Rumilly.

Before crossing the Aa, turn right on to a tarred path, then turn left on to the D132 before rejoining the D148. After 200 metres the GR path turns left up the D129E towards Herly. About 2 kilometres farther on, at a left-hand bend on the top of the hill, the GR keeps straight on south westwards along a grassy path which then comes down steeply below a thicket, crosses a seasonal stream bed and climbs again on a good gravelled track along the dry valley. At the crossroads with the D156 the GR heads left along the road and then, at the top of a short climb, takes the right-hand fork along a tarred path, and after 150 metres bears right again, heading west—south-west along a dirt track between hedges, skirting the meadows of the village of Herly.

The GR then rejoins the D129E road, following it to the right for 300 metres to the first houses of Avesnes.

The GR takes a hedge-lined tarmac path to the left, then turns right along a tarred track — with unclear waymarking — at first through a cutting but then gradually climbing in a south-westerly direction. Ceasing to be surfaced, and again unclearly marked, it forks left at a Y-shaped junction and continues its climb to the cross-roads with the D343, at an altitude of 190 metres.

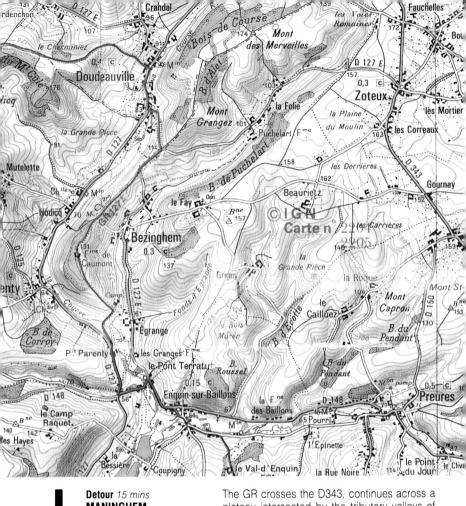

Detour *15 mins*
MANINGHEM
♈

*Turn right and follow the
D343 for 1 kilometre.*

QUILEN
♈

*Notice the huge timber-raft
in the centre of the village,
one of the last of its kind.*

2.5Km
0:35

The GR crosses the D343, continues across a
plateau intersected by the tributary valleys of
the Canche, and descends on a fine gravelled
path to Quilen.

The GR route passes to the right of the timber-
raft, crosses the D129E road, and climbs
rapidly west-north-west along a tarred, and
then gravelled, track, skirting the Quilen woods.
Passing two turnings off to the left, the GR
crosses the busy D126 near a wayside Calvary
and keeps straight ahead along a barely
discernible dirt trail which soon enters the
woods. You then start to descend more and
more steeply. Ignore several turnings on both
sides and follow the waymarking carefully,
then swing sharply right, and come out of the
woods on to a country road, which brings you

to the D152E. Follow this to the left and into Bimont.

BIMONT
♟

5.3Km
1:20

Detour *30 mins*
HUCQUELIERS
✕ ♟ ⛴ 🚌

'Capital' of the 'Haut-Pays' —'High-Country'; church, town square, craft shop. Turn left along the D128 for 2 kilometres.

Detour *35 mins*
PREURES
✕ ♟ 🚌

Museum and Merovingian cemetery. Turn right and follow the D150 for 2.4 kilometres.

The GR leaves the D152E at the church and climbs steeply up a poorly cleared pathway which joins a gravelled track 150 metres east of the remote Plouy farm.

Warning From the reverse direction take careful note of the waymarking.

The GR joins the D152 and continues along it to the right for some 200 metres, then turns left onto a tarred track through open country. After another kilometre, at the eastern arm of Bois Noël, it comes to a complicated six-way crossroads — note the waymarking carefully.

The GR takes the second road to the left, the D151 towards Alette and Montcavrel, skirting the southern edge of the trees, then follows a tarred track to the right, heading northwest. Some 1.2 kilometres farther on it comes to the D150, close to the hamlet of Le Fayel de Preures.

Turn right on to the D150 and leave it again almost immediately for a dirt track on the left. After 400 metres bear right. The partly gravelled footpath goes gently down, with some good views, towards the Baillons valley. A little way past a derelict motor car the trail disappears for 50 metres and then carries on down a wide gravelled country track.

Warning Coming in the reverse direction there is an enormous risk of missing the turning, since the above-mentioned country track continues on a long way southwards, but this is not shown on the maps, nor on the land survey, and the gap in the path makes it difficult to spot the dirt trail which the GR uses.

The country track goes down through woods to the remote farm at Le Val d'Enquin.

Val d'Enquin

1.2Km
0:20

The GR then follows a tarred path down into the Baillons valley, where it turns left on to another such path alongside a fish farm, and comes to Enquins-sur-Baillons.

139

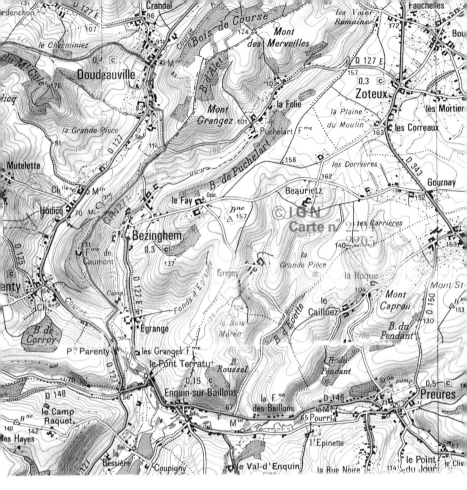

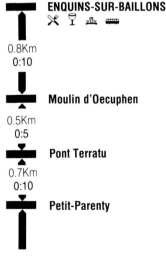

ENQUINS-SUR-BAILLONS

0.8Km
0:10

Moulin d'Oecuphen

0.5Km
0:5

Pont Terratu

0.7Km
0:10

Petit-Parenty

The GR crosses the River Baillons, goes left towards the church and little 18th-century château, and meets the D148, which it follows to the left for 700 metres alongside the water-cress beds to the hamlet of Le Moulin

The footpath continues to the left along the D148, crosses the River Course and comes to the crossroads at the hamlet of Pont Terratu.

The GR footpath then turns right on to the busy D127 road as far as the hamlet of Petit Parenty.

Here the GR takes a gravelled track to the right, heading north, crosses the Course, then climbs above the valley of Bezinghem stream, before turning left up a steep track which

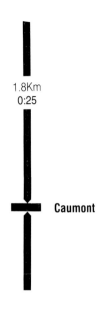

1.8Km
0:25

Caumont

disappears after some 300 metres, leaving only a vague outline in the grass. You should keep heading north-west without turning right, as waymarking is unclear. After another 200 metres the line seems to get lost in a clump of sloe bushes on the edge of the Bois de Caumont. Keep straight on through the thick brushwood and within 15 metres you come out on an overgrown forest ride, followed by a more obvious trail through the underbrush of a beech-wood, leading to the isolated farm at Caumont.

Here the GR continues along the tarmac track to the left of the farm.

Caution Coming in the reverse direction the way in to the forest trail is to the right of the farm garage, after skirting the buildings for some 50 metres.

Notre Dame de Lorett

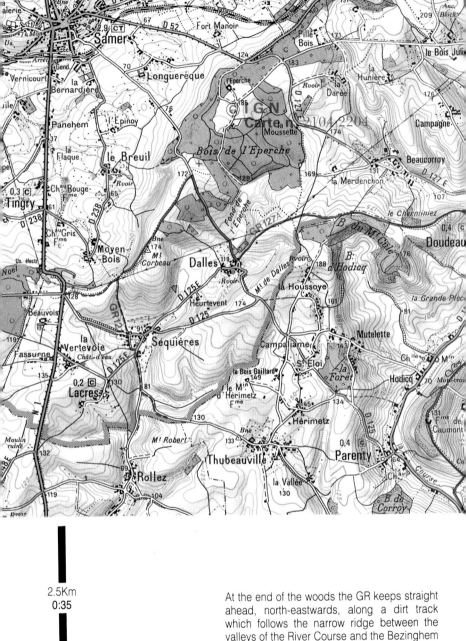

2.5Km
0:35

At the end of the woods the GR keeps straight ahead, north-eastwards, along a dirt track which follows the narrow ridge between the valleys of the River Course and the Bezinghem stream.

Detour *10 mins*
BEZINGHEM
▲ 🍷
Follow the tarmac path to the right for 700 metres.

From here the GR carries on to meet and follow the D127E north-westwards, to a cross-roads, where it turns left down to the village of Doudeauville.

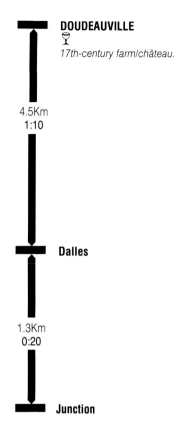

DOUDEAUVILLE

17th-century farm/château.

4.5Km
1:10

Dalles

1.3Km
0:20

Junction

Detour *35 mins*
SAMER

After following the D127 north through the village for 500 metres, the GR takes a gravelled country track to the left, climbing northwest. At the second turning the footpath swings westwards, still climbing, above a small dry valley, with a view of the medieval motte at Crandal. It runs alongside a wood on the right, and then comes to a crossways at the edge of the Mont-Culé wood. Keep straight on towards the west on a semi-overgrown path which passes to the right of the wood, with unclear waymarking. The GR then joins a gravelled track climbing up from the right and follows it, still heading west. It crosses another track and then drops down towards the little hamlet of Dalles.

The GR footpath here makes a sharp turn to the right, on to tarred track.

Caution Waymarking unclear from the reverse direction.

After a short descent this climbs to the high ground on the rim of the Boulonnais lowland. Beyond a small wood you come to spot height 172 metres, and meet the path linking the GRs 120 and 121.

The GR127A joins the link path which branches to the right to the GR120, and to the left to the GR121 see pages 59 and 175.

Detour, see left. From the junction continue on the tarred track, heading north-west for 2.5 kilometres.

GR127B; DENNEBROEUCQ–BRUNEMBERT

Junction

From the junction, the GR127B turns onto the unsurfaced track to the right. After 300 metres the track is broken by land management operations, but a narrow bank on the edge of a field, heading north-east, has been spared, and can be used for 400 metres to reach a cart track, where you turn sharp left. After a hedge take the second track on the right, slanting towards the north-west. It crosses the D133 and climbs steeply uphill.

Detour *15 mins*
AUDINCTHUN

Turn right along the D133 for 1 kilometre.

A little farther on the GR turns left along the D92 for 180 metres to the top of Mont Roblin, where there are extensive views eastwards over the Lys valley and westwards over the Aa valley.

Detour *30 mins*
FAUQUEMBERGUES

6.7Km
1:35

Continue along the D92 for 2 kilometres.

The GR footpath turns right along a tarmac track to Mont-Saint-Liévin farm at 185 metres altitude. It skirts round the farm to the west and forks right down an unsurfaced path, which is overgrown for 200 metres, and crosses the D158 road.

Caution Walking in the reverse direction: From the crossing with the D158, take the barely discernible path in the grass, *not* the splendid gravelled track a little to its left. The waymarking here is unclear.

Beyond the D158, the GR footpath is gravel. Some 300 metres farther on, it turns left, heading north west, the surface changes to tarmac, and the path drops down to the hamlet of Bout-de-la-Ville in the Aa valley, crossing the D928 on the way.

Bout-de-la-Ville
Detour *20 mins*
FAUQUEMBERGUES

Can also be reached from Bout-de-la-Ville: 1.5 kilometres along the D928 to the left.

The GR continues along a little road to the right for 150 metres, then forks right up a steeply climbing gravel track to the right of a chalk-marl quarry, then heads north east across the bare plateau. Two side turnings come in from the left in the space of 1,500 metres, and the GR takes the second of these, slanting back to the left (almost a full half turn)

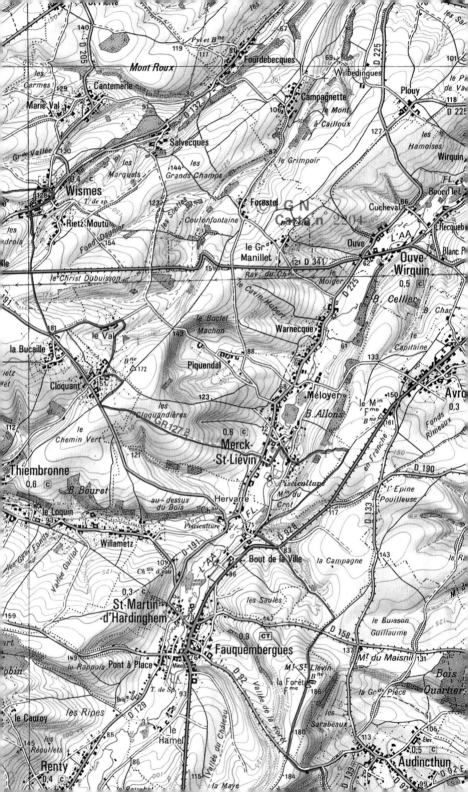

2.8Km
0:40

MERCK-SAINT-LIÉVIN
⛺ ✕ 🍷 ⚓ 🚌
*Interesting church dating
from 16th and 17th
centuries; bell-tower.*

4Km
1

Cloquant

1.2Km
0:20

Le Val

2.8Km
0:40

WISMES
🍷 ⚓
Interesting church.

to head west south-west.

Warning This section is out in open country and the waymarking is unclear. The route becomes difficult to make out on the high ground, where there is some ploughing in places.

The footpath runs along a hedge and then cuts through a narrow, overgrown stretch down a steep incline, bringing you along a more obvious trail to Merck-Saint-Liévin.

The GR goes left from the church, past the cemetery, along a tarred road for 500 metres, then turns right down a gravelled track leading to a mill on the Aa (a view of the church from this interesting spot). Go through the fish farm and cross the D225 — dog-leg right and then left. The path climbs gently up the western side of the valley, first on tarmac, then on gravel and finally bare earth, to join the D191, turning right and then immediately right again on to an earth path alongside some hedges on the outskirts of a hamlet. After an overgrown stretch of some 200 metres you reach a crossways, where a tarmac track leads left into the hamlet, Cloquant.

At the next farm take an earth path to the right. This joins a track which is at first gravel, then grassy, and crosses a hollow. Then take a tarmac path to the left at the outskirts of the hamlet of Le Val.

The tarmac path climbs gently and joins the D191 near La Bucaille hamlet. Turn right on to a re-aligned, newly re-surfaced path which crosses the D341, — the old Roman road from Arras to Boulogne — at the 186 metres marker.
Go due north down a path, gravelled at first and then unsurfaced, which then climbs for a short stretch and brings you to Wismes.

The GR footpath crosses the D132 road without entering the village, then turns left along a track which is at first gravelled and then runs through grass, heading west. The route takes you across a rather uniform stretch of plateau, crosses the D191, and after 100 metres comes to a partly-gravel track.

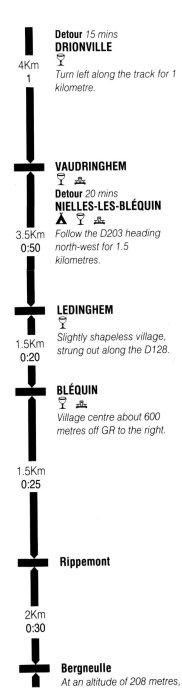

Detour *15 mins*
DRIONVILLE
♟

4Km
1

Turn left along the track for 1 kilometre.

VAUDRINGHEM
♟ ⚒

Detour *20 mins*
NIELLES-LES-BLÉQUIN
▲ ♟ ⚒

3.5Km
0:50

Follow the D203 heading north-west for 1.5 kilometres.

LEDINGHEM
♟

1.5Km
0:20

Slightly shapeless village, strung out along the D128.

BLÉQUIN
♟ ⚒

Village centre about 600 metres off GR to the right.

1.5Km
0:25

Rippemont

2Km
0:30

Bergneulle
At an altitude of 208 metres,

The GR turns right along the track, crosses the D131 and comes to a wayside cross on the Mont de Drionville, altitude 188 metres. It then goes down to Vaudringhem, joins a gravelled track and then turns immediately right down a gently sloping bare earth track. This crosses the D203E and runs alongside a hedge. After another 200 metres it turns left down a twisting tarmac path to Vaudringhem.

Skirt around Vaudringhem church — two right turns — and then head left along the D203 road. After 400 metres turn off right on a tarred track down a small valley. Beyond the bridge turn left up an earth path which heads southwest, climbing gradually to the top of a spur with the Bléquin valley to the right, the Floyecques valley to the left. At the second crossroads, 2 kilometres farther on, take the right-hand tarmac path down to Ledinghem.

Cross the D128 and follow a gently climbing tarmac path, then turn right along a steep, partly-made up track. The GR crosses a track at the top of the rise and comes down again to the outskirts of Bléquin.

Turn left along the road, after 500 metres turn right, cross the Bléquin stream and join the D202. At this intersection take a barely discernible path to the left, alongside a hedge. This is a tricky section. Look for a recent clearing newly planted with trees. The GR footpath slants back by way of a left-hand hairpin bend, some 400 metres farther on, onto a tarred minor road which you follow to the right to the hamlet of Rippemont. Note: This is a temporary situation pending complete clearance of the track just mentioned.

Go to the right along a partly-made up grassy track which climbs the Mont de Rippemont, altitude 193 metres, makes a sharp turn and comes down in a northerly direction into a valley, where it joins the D202. Continue left along this road for a kilometre to the isolated farm at Bergneulle.

The GR follows the D254 to the right for another kilometre and then, at a left-hand

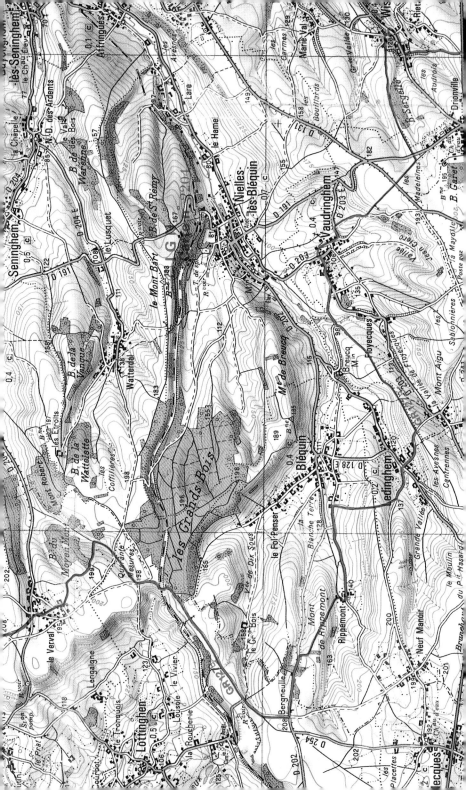

this is known as the 'roof' of the Pas de Calais.

bend, keeps straight on along a tarmac path heading north-east. This path, gravelled later on, follows the southern edge of the Boulonnais Weald. It offers extensive views, to the left over the low-lying areas and to the right over the artesian plateau intersected by the tributaries of the Aa. On the left you can also see remains of the old railway extension which clambered up to German military installations that were hidden in Mont Fauclin woods, to the right of the path.

5.5Km
1:20

You cross the disused Boulogne to Saint-Omer railway line, go straight ahead at a fork and come to an intersection with a tarmac path. At this point you are at the junction of the northern and southern rims of the Boulonnais Weald. When walking in the reverse direction, take the right-hand path. After another 50 metres the GR goes right, north-east along an unsurfaced path across fields, with unclear waymarking, joins a gravelled track for 100 metres and then goes down a combe with waymarking unclear; follow the direction of steepest slope). In another 300 metres the GR turns left up a near-derelict track which crosses another track on the edge of a wood. From here the route down into another hollow is more obvious. It then takes a left-hand fork along a gravelled track to the farms at Le Verval.

Le Verval

Turn on to a tarred track to the right, north-west, and then leave it to carry on straight ahead along an unsurfaced extension which joins up with another road and comes out to the D204 beside the village chapel. Turn left and immediately right along a gravelled track running north-west with hedges on either side. This joins another gravelled track which you follow for 100 metres to the right as far as a Calvary at spot height 208, then fork left along an earth track. After 300 metres, at a crossroads in open country, with no waymarking, turn left along another earth track heading south-west, which climbs gently, crosses a gravelled track and then runs down the northern lip of the valley. The track becomes gravelled and then, at the level of the source of the river Liane, tarred, as it brings you to Quesques.

2.5Km
0:35

QUESQUES

Turn right on to the D245E road and keep straight on along a gently climbing tarred road. After 150 metres turn left along an unsurfaced track flanked by a hedge. This path crosses a tarred track on to which you turn right, heading north-north-east. You then cross the aforementioned tarred road and the GR climbs to a saddle marking the route to Escoeuilles. At the top the GR follows the bare earth path to the left, heading north-west.

5.2Km
1:20

ESCOEUILLES
Detour *15 mins*

Continue straight ahead down the track for 1 kilometre.

At the second crossroads the footpath bears left alongside a strange wooded blind valley known as 'la Fosse' or 'la Creuse' — the Pit or Hollow, which local legend associates with the giant Gargantua. The route then heads south-west down the side of Mont de Brunembert and meets a tarred track, turning right on to it and continuing to the crossroads with the D215. Turn left on to this road for 300 metres. On the outskirts of Brunembert a tarred track to the right brings you to the GR120 in 200 metres; see page 173.

Junction
The GR127 meets the GR120.

BRUNEMBERT
Detour *5 mins*

Keep left, south-west, along the D215 for 500 metres.

LINK PATH BETWEEN GR127 BOURS AND GR121A ST-POL-SUR-TERNOISE

This link path is 15.7 kilometres long, running north–south, crossing the northern part of the Ternois uplands. It makes it possible to complete a circular tour using both the GR121 and the GR127 in three or four days starting from Arras. There is another circular walk from the Boulonnais, using the GRs 121, 121A, 127 and 120. The starting point of the link path is at Bours, near the railway halt.

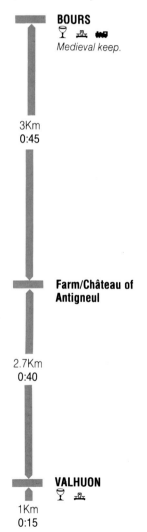

BOURS

Medieval keep.

3Km
0:45

Farm/Château of Antigneul

2.7Km
0:40

VALHUON

1Km
0:15

Some 100 metres beyond the tunnel under the railway, the GR127 turns right, due north along the railway halt approach. At this same intersection the link path turns in the opposite direction, to the left and due south, along a tarred path which eventually becomes a rather muddy track. On coming to the D89 you turn left along it towards Diéval for 400 metres **Caution** Waymarking unclear coming from the reverse direction. Continue for 200 metres beyond the railway bridge, the link path then turns right on to a tarmac path going southeast. This climbs quickly up to the Mont de Monneville and continues south along a gravelled track. After climbing gently alongside a wood, the link path turns right along another gravelled track to the farm/château of Antigneul, set among wide drives of beech trees.

Follow the tarred track running due south from the farm for 200 metres, and turn right along a path beside a wood where the waymarking is hard to see. This joins a partly-gravelled track going north-westwards, and crosses a railway line.

The link path keeps going towards the northwest for a kilometre and then forks to the left, westwards, on a level with a solitary bush. It crosses another track some 300 metres farther on, leaves the open fields and runs alongside hedges on the outskirts of Valhuon, and joins the D77.

The route keeps to the D77, heading right, for 50 metres, and then takes a little narrow street to the left which comes to a small square. Go left again along an earth path between

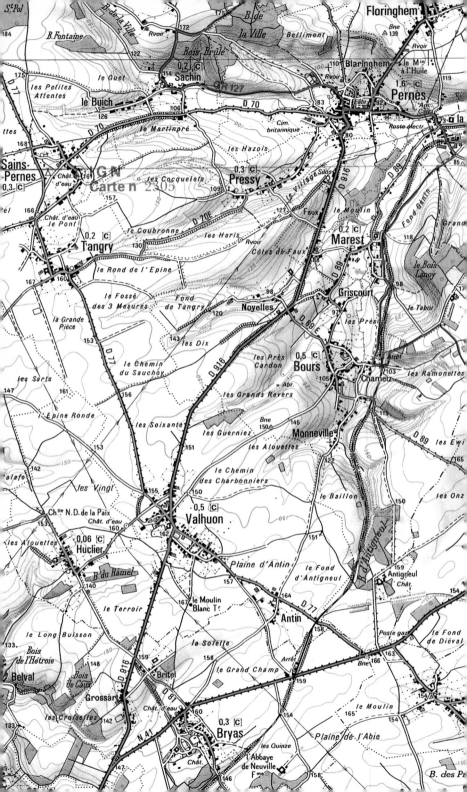

hedges, which runs south–south-west and comes to Moulin Blanc.

Moulin Blanc

A ruined but still imposing mill. Spot height 167, one of the highest points in the Ternois.

2.3Km
0:35

The link path then turns sharp right, to the north-west, and after 500 metres crosses the D916, which is another way into Valhoun. The next 200 metres are muddy, with hedges each side, but then a better path keeps going north-west — a typical 'round the houses' Ternois village walk — which brings you to the D88 near a water tower. Go left along this road to Huclier.

Huclier

2.2Km
0:35

From here the link path goes right and then left to the church, along a gravelled track sloping steeply down to the south-west. Turn left after 500 metres on to a grass path running along above Belval.

Belval hamlet and monastery

The present monastery is a recent structure. Remains of the 18th-century building visible a little lower down along the D87.
Farm produce is displayed and sold, including some noteworthy cheeses.

2.2Km
0:35

The link path goes along the D87 to the right, past the monastery, and 300 metres farther on goes left on to a path running due south, tarred at first but eventually unsurfaced, which climbs gently to Troisvaux chapel.

Troisvaux Chapel

Altitude 145 metres. Fine view over the Ternois uplands and the Ternoise valley.

1Km
0:15

The link path goes to the left of the chapel on a grass path heading south, which is partly sunken. **Warning** Coming from the reverse direction, heading towards Belval, the way-marking is unclear. After 500 metres you cross another, better maintained path, and head south-east on a gently climbing but barely discernible track to meet the D87 at spot height 138.7, and turn right along the road. This is another stretch which is difficult to make out from the reverse direction. The route takes you through the hamlet of Rosemont.

Rosemont

1.3Km
0:20

Just beyond the Ternois clinic the GR bears to the right along an almost flat earth trail which then dips, skirts an allotment and comes out into Saint-Pol by way of the Rue de Conteville **Warning** the starting point of this pathway is hard to spot from the reverse direction.

SAINT-POL-SUR-TERNOISE

At the foot of the Rue de Conteville, the link path joins the Rue d'Aire and the GR121A, which runs to the right heading towards the Ternoise, Anvin and the Forest of Hesdin; and to the left skirts St-Pol heading for Flers and the Canche valley.

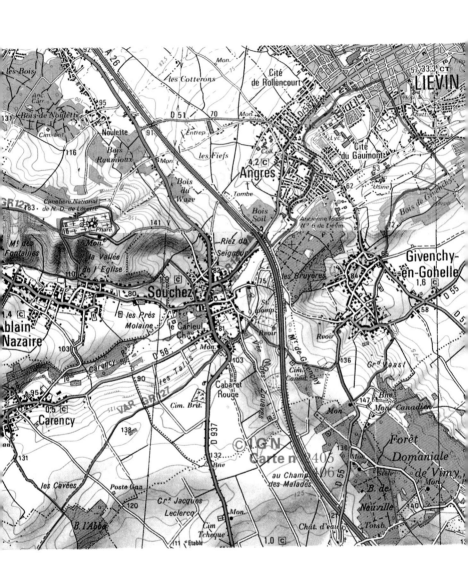

LE CIRCUIT DES COLLINES DE GOHELLE

The Gohelle Hills variant is 18.75 kilometres long. By using part of the main GR127 to join up the ends, you can complete a circular tour of 23.75 kilometres.

This circular route offers a brief introduction to the Gohelle district, a vast, history-laden territory extending between the Audomarois and Douaisois regions, parallel to the hills of Artois, and bounded by the Pas-de-Calais mining district. The variant also gives access to the GR127 from the mining area, in particular from Lens and Liévin.

Its starting point is Bois l'Abbé, between Mont Saint-Eloi and Carency, about 10 kilometres from the start of the GR127 footpath; see page 115.

Bois l'Abbé

The Gohelle variant leaves the GR127 some 50 metres north-west of Bois l'Abbé, turning right. A gently climbing unsurfaced path heads north-east and after 500 metres crosses a tarred track. At spot height 136 it crosses another earth track and continues north-east. Heading gently downhill, with a view over the Souchez valley, it crosses two more paths, passes to the left of the Cabaret Rouge military cemetery, becomes tarred, and draws level with the district cemetery on the outskirts of Souchez. Note the memorial to General Barbot and the Chasseurs Alpins, in memory of the battles of May 1915.

3.25Km
0:50

SOUCHEZ

The GR crosses the D937 road, goes down a tarred path, and 300 metres farther on heads north-east along a path across the 'Vallée des Zouaves'. A few metres before reaching a pumping station, the path forks right along a gravelled track heading south-east, which climbs up the so-called 'Fontaine des Écouloirs', the final ridge of the Artois on the edge of the great North European Plain. The GR goes through a tunnel under the A26 motorway. On leaving the tunnel you turn right, south-eastwards along a path through meadows, cross the Mont de Givenchy and eventually turn right on to the D55 to reach the Moroccan Memorial.

2.5Km
0:35

Memorial to the Moroccan Division
From some way off the Vimy Canadian Memorial will have been visible.

Detour 5 mins

Vimy Canadian Memorial

This memorial, 400 metres off the GR, stands on territory granted by France to Canada in memory of the 64,000 Canadian soldiers who fell during the 1914–18 war. It stands at spot height 140, one of the most fiercely contended points in the campaign of April 1917. The memorial, which represents the gates of immortality, was unveiled in 1936.
From the terrace surrounding the monument there is a fine view over the farmlands of the Gohelle plain and the mining area around Liévin, Lens and Avion.

2.75Km
0:40

From the Memorial to the Moroccan Division, turn left along the tarred road described as 'panoramic' which heads north-east, passing round the Canadian memorial to the left. Since you are on Canadian soil, there can be no waymarking. After 300 metres, just before a right-hand bend, look out for a little sunken path on the left, down the escarpment slope of the main Artois fault. This brings you to the large villge of Givenchy-en-Gohelle.

GIVENCHY-EN-GOHELLE
🍷 ⚒

3Km
0:45

Go right through Givenchy keeping on a north–south heading to the 'Place d'Or' on the D51 road. The route leads through a variety of streets and paths on the way, so keep an eye on the waymarking. From the 'Place d'Or', take a road to the right towards the 'Sablière de Liévin' (Liévin sand pit). Here you cross an old spoil tip which formed the embankment for a railway carrying coal from the Angres depression to the washing-plant at Liévin.

Warning Follow the waymarking carefully which leads through the town of Liévin.

LIÉVIN
🍴 🍷 ⚒ 🚌

This huge industrial conurbation has its origins in mining. It was totally rebuilt after 1918, and consists of town centres clustered around an administrative and commercial centre. The GR runs through this centre to reach the Hôtel de Ville — the town hall.

1.5Km
0:20

From the Hôtel de Ville the GR heads south-west along the River Souchez, through green parkland called the 'Equipages', once a farm and stables belonging to the mines at Liévin, and then the 'Parc de Rollencourt', site of a medieval castle destroyed in the 1914–18 war, which is now a sports stadium. Pay close attention to the waymarking. Keep alongside the Souchez and this brings you to Anaves.

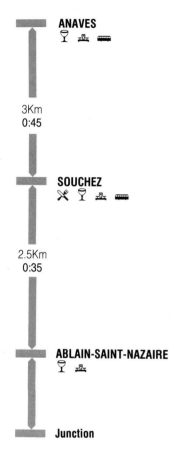

ANAVES

3Km
0:45

SOUCHEZ

2.5Km
0:35

ABLAIN-SAINT-NAZAIRE

Junction

On reaching the end of the path along the Souchez, the GR turns left along a street for some 200 metres, then goes down a flight of steps to the right, meeting the Souchez again. Follow the waymarking carefully to the 'Chemin des Normands', a path between Souchez and Liévin which has been shown on maps of the area since 1749. The A26 motorway cuts across it. Take a recently completed diversion, and then turn left on to the D58 road which brings you back to Souchez.

Leaving the D58 road, the GR crosses the site of the old village, which was totally destroyed in 1915. Follow the waymarking there carefully. The GR then crosses the D937 again at the level of the main square, follows the D57 for 150 metres and then turns right, due north, up a street which climbs gently through a housing estate. After bearing north-west it becomes an unsurfaced track and turns left along another dirt road, heading south-west, which skirts the foot of Lorette hill and runs down towards Ablain-Saint-Nazaire.

For a moment the GR overlooks the ruins of the flamboyant Gothic church which was destroyed in 1915. It then climbs again to rejoin the main GR127 at a placed called the 'Mont de Justice', spot height 110.

The Gohelle Hills variant joins the main GR127, which leads to the right to the Boulonnais, and to the left to Louez and Arras — or back to the starting point of the variant at Bois l'Abbé.

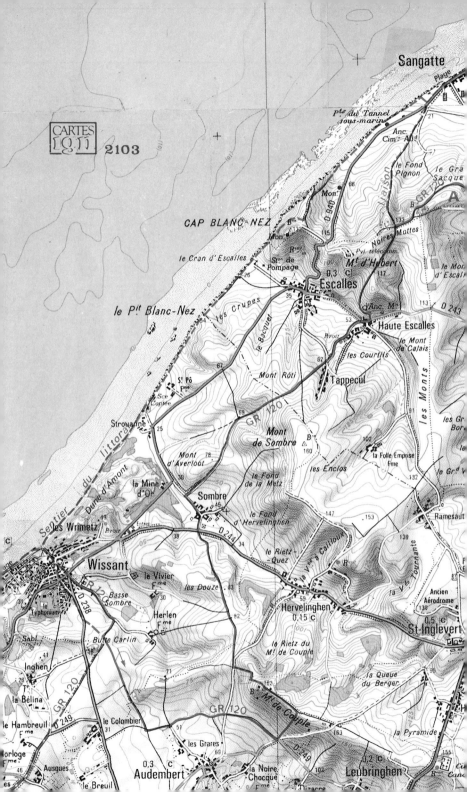

WALK 5

WISSANT

⌂ ⛺ ✕ 🍷 ⛴ 🚃
ℹ️

*Beach centrally located
between the two capes,
Gris-Nez and Blanc-Nez, the
first area to be designated as
a site of major national
importance.*

6Km
1:30

Mont de Couple
161m
*View across both capes, the
straits of the Pas-de-Calais
and the surrounding
countryside.*

3Km
0:45

Sombre

4Km
1

Haute-Escalles
Detour *15 mins*
ESCALLES
⌂ ⛺ ✕ 🍷 🚃
*Go left along the D243
road at the intersection.*
Detour *40 mins*
Cap Blanc-Nez
*View point; Coastal footpath;
International Cross-Channel*

1.5Km
0:20

The GR120 footpath starts from the church
and crosses the D940 road heading south-
east. It follows a made up road in the direction
of Herlen. A little way past a statue of the
Virgin Mary on the left-hand side of the road,
take the right fork and go up a gravelled track.
At the first crossroads go left along a service
track with unclear waymarking for about 1,500
metres, and on reaching another crossroads
turn left, to the east. Cross over 2 tarred roads
and skirt the foot of Mont de Couple, leaving
Audembert village behind you on your right.
On coming to the intersection with the D249 do
not go along the road, but, instead, take 2
turnings to the left and go up a grass path
across a heath to the summit of Mont de
Couple. On reaching the top, take the gravelled track left along the ridge.

Near the blockhouses head north—north-west
and starting down, go round to the right of a
copse and join a tarred road. Follow the road
for about 100 metres to the right and then bear
left on to a dirt path. The GR crosses the
D244 road and brings you to the hamlet of
Sombre.

The footpath turns left in this tiny village and in
another 300 metres heads north-east along a
made up road which eventually becomes a
stone track. Keep heading north-east along
the same path to a place called Le Tappecul.
At the fork take the road heading north-east
and pass a barn on your left. This brings you
to Haute-Escalles.

Detour see left. From Escalles, turn to the right
along the D940 as far as spot height 114.
Follow a footpath to the left leading to the
Dover Patrol Memorial.

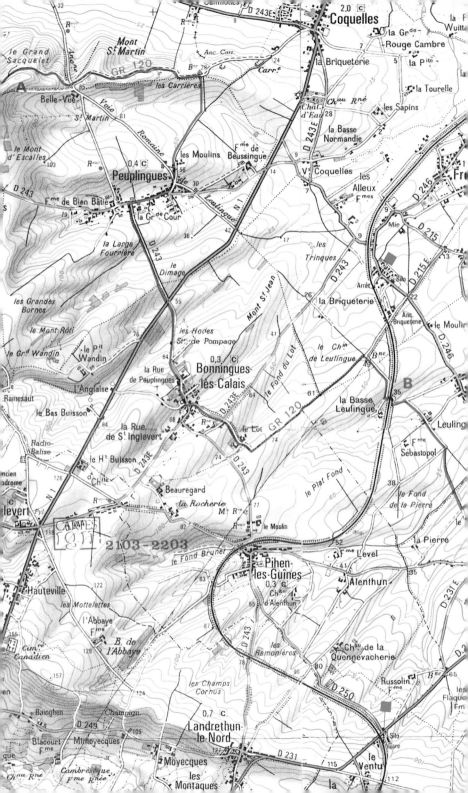

Cap Blanc-Nez

The Cape is part of the 'Two Capes' designated site and the Boulonnais Regional Nature Park. This is the first area in France to have been afforded the protection and management of a national site, recognizing the value of the cliffs, dunes, marshes and estuaries which make up this area of coastline.

Furthermore, the Boulonnais Regional Nature Park, founded by the Nord-Pas-de-Calais Region, is responsible for conserving and making the most of the coastline and countryside, conducting rural development programmes, promoting tourist facilities and cultural activities, and developing a range of educational material, information services and environmental protection measures.

Cap Blanc-Nez marks the north-eastern extremity of Wissant Bay, and rises to 130 metres above sea level. It consists mainly of chalk, and was formed some 100 million years ago at a time when the Continent was under the sea.

On the summit of the headland an orienting table helps you to identify your surroundings: sandy Wissant Bay, the Flemish coastal plain to the east, the rural hinterland and, on a clear day, the English coast.

Museum dealing with all schemes for crossing the Channel.

1.5Km
0:20

Noires Mottes

Views of the North Sea and the Channel Tunnel construction site; now the edge of a cliff overlooking the coastal plain of the Calais region, but once, several thousand years ago, the sea actually lapped at its base.

Detour *45 mins*
SANGATTE
Y ⚓ 🚌

Town square; coastal footpath.
Head north along a track on the left as far as the D940, which leads to this place.

Turn to the right along the D243 for about 100 metres and then turn left up a made up path which takes you past an old mill. You then come to the highest point of the Noires Mottes.

Descend for about 50 metres as far as spot height 132.

At spot height 132, turn right on to a gravelled track. Bear north-east between 2 shrub-covered hills and continue north-east along a track which is grassy at first and then gravelled. Cross a metalled road known as the 'Chemin de Leulingue' on the line of an old Roman road. Carry straight on eastwards along a gravelled track, and then through a quarry area. The GR turns right, heading due south.

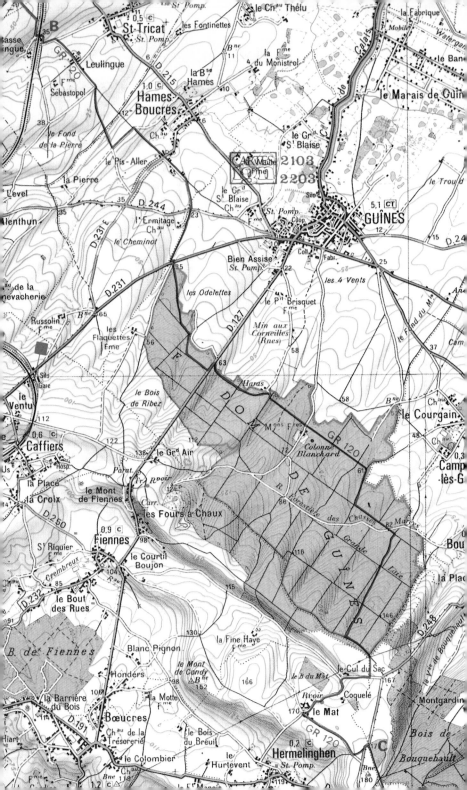

Detour *30mins*
Maison du Marbre et de la Géologie
The House of Marble and Geology in the Bassin Canver, Marquise.

Detour *30 mins*
COQUELLES
⚒
Windmill in working order.

4Km
1

Detour
CALAIS
🏨 ⌂ ✕ 🍷 ⚒ 🚌
🚐

5 kilometres from Coquelles. Statue of the Burghers of Calais by the sculptor Rodin; Hôtel de Ville, 15th century Flemish style, with belltower; Place d'Armes, parade square with 13th century watchtower; Citadel with 17th century bastions.

PEUPLINGUES
⌂ ⛺ 🍷

6.5Km
1:40

Leulingue

2.5Km
0:40

Detour see left. From the point where the GR turns due south, some 2 kilometres from the Noire Mottes, continue along the track, heading north and then east. The track joins a road to the village.

The GR120 turns right, heading due south. A little farther on, bear right and come to Peuplingues.

At the outskirts of the village follow the D243, bearing slightly to the right, for 700 metres, then turn left, still following the road as far as Bonningues-les-Calais. At the centre of Bonningues-les-Calais turn left, cross the D243E, and beyond the place called Le Lot, turn to the left and follow the footpath for 2 kilometres. At spot height 49 close to the triangulation point, turn to the right under an overhead power line. A little farther on the GR turns parallel with a railway line before crossing under it through a tunnel on the left. In another 100 metres take the north-east fork, then turn right towards the south-east, keeping all the while to the road. This road goes through the hamlet of Leulingue.

The GR continues, and at the first right-angled bend on the right, turns left off the road and follows a gravelled track with unclear waymarking. Take the second track on the left and in another 500 metres turn right at right-angles south-eastwards along one edge of an overgrown sunken lane. This brings you to the

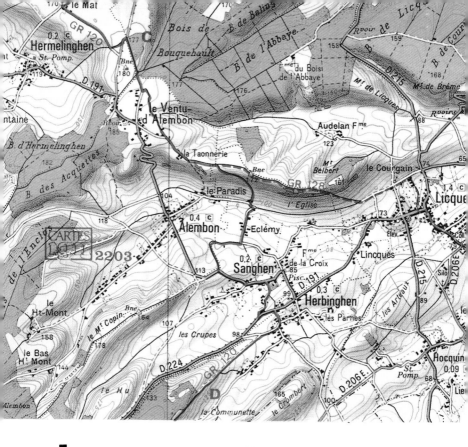

outskirts of Hames-Boucres village.

Hames-Boucres
Detour *15 mins*
HAMES-BOUCRES CENTRE

Detour *40 mins*
CHÂTEAU THÉLU

1.5Km
0:20

Detour see left. Go left along the D231E road at the intersection.

Detour see left. In the centre of Hames-Boucres turn left along the D215 for about 50 metres, then turn right and stay on the road as far as spot height 10, where you go obliquely left.

After crossing the D231E road, the GR follows the line of a minor made up road for 900 metres. After crossing the D244, it skirts the left hand side of a nursery of young trees and then follows a dirt path as far as the D231. It makes a brief detour left along this road, then turns right and reaches the State forest of Guînes.

State forest of Guînes

Detour *30 mins*

GUÎNES

🏠 ⛺ ✕ ♟ 🚃 🚌

Ancient fortified castle; nearby, the Field of the Cloth of Gold, scene of the famous meeting in 1520 between François I of France and Henry VIII of England.

4.5Km
1

FOREST LODGE AT CAMPAGNE-LÈS-GUÎNES

⛺

Look for the Blanchard column, marking the spot where Blanchard and Jefferies landed by balloon on 7 January 1785 after becoming the first ever to cross the Channel by air.

5Km
1:15

Le Cul de Sac

Detour

HERMELINGHEN

🏠

Where the GR turns left beyond Le Mat farm continue straight on, following the road to Hermelinghen.

3Km
0:45

Le Ventu d'Alembon

Detour see left. Either take the D244 road left at the crossroads near the young trees, or go left along the D231 at the next intersection.

From the D231 road the GR follows a narrow tarred road for a dozen metres. Then go left at an angle along a service ride into the forest proper. The pathway skirts the north-eastern edge of the forest as far as the forest lodge.

Warning Take care in the forest. Forestry operations may lead to changes in the route, so pay particular attention to the waymarkings.

From the forest lodge, turn to the right along a well kept pathway to spot height 61. Turn right and keep going to the southern edge of the forest at a place called Le Cul de Sac.

Go to the right and follow a winding made up road. Turn left beyond Le Mat farm.

In another 800 metres or so, turn left off the road on to a dirt track. Cross over the tarred road at spot height 177 and turn to the right along a track beside the woods. This brings you eventually to a gravelled track with unclear waymarking through the fields. Go left along here and skirt the village called Le Ventu d'Alembon.

The GR then follows the barbed wire fence along the hedge. It comes to a narrow, made up minor road and follows it to the left past La Taonnerie farm. At the end of the hedge go to the right down a steep grassy path into the Pays de Licques valley. This brings you to a made up road with a hairpin bend at Eclemy

5Km
1:15

SANGHEN
Fish breeding can be seen.
Detour *30 mins*
LICQUES

1Km
0:15

HERBINGHEN
Church dating back to 1740.

6.5Km
1:40

N42 and CD206 Crossroads
We meet the cuesta formation with Lower Boulonnais at its foot. The countryside in Lower Boulonnais is mainly a mixture of woodland and pasture, devoted above all to livestock farming, horses, cattle, sheep, pigs, etc.
Detour
NABRINGHEN

Follow the N42 to the right from the crossroads.

There are quarries of red,

hamlet. In another 500 metres leave this road at a right-angled bend and take a track on the right which at first runs between hedges and then crosses the fields. The GR then meets a road to be followed to the left to Sanghen.

Detour see left. Go back up the road some 50 metres from the fish hatchery. Turn right and keep on for the village, past the church and a wayside calvary.

By the school, turn right at right angles southwards and follow a path to a tarred road. Turn left and follow the road for about 50 metres, then turn immediately right on to a sunken track leading to Herbinghen.

The footpath turns right twice, and then in another 500 metres goes at an angle south-west, to the left, along a gravelled track. It skirts a wood and then crosses it to a place called Les Sarts, spot height 190. Cross the D224, and keep straight on along a service track leading to Mont Dauphin where there is a panoramic view. Turn left and cross back over the D224 road at spot height 200, taking a gravelled track which winds across the hillside to the crossroads.

From here, turn left, towards Licques, walk about 40 metres along the D206 road and turn off to the left along a grass path to Labiette hamlet. You reach a tarred road. At the intersection turn right as far as the D206, crossing it and taking a path which comes to the N42 at La Converserie in the commune district of Longueville. The footpath crosses the Route Nationale and keeps straight on along a tarmac road. At the next crossroads go left for about 100 metres and continue straight ahead towards the hamlet of Le Hamel.

white and mauve banded clay still operating. They are used in the manufacture of tiles and bricks.

Junction

6.5Km
1:40

At Hamel the GR120 bears right along a made up track. The tarmac road continues straight ahead to the D215 road where it meets the GR127B.

In another 500 metres the GR120 turns right again, passing a transformer, and just beyond it leaves the road for a grassy path leading to grazing land. Cross this meadow and come to the D252 road, following it to the right to the commune of Brunembert.

Brunembert
Detour *10 mins*
BRUNEMBERT VILLAGE
� ⚱

3Km
0:45

Go left along the D252 road for 500 metres.

At the intersection, go left along the D253E heading for Henneveux. At the next wayside calvary, spot height 107, keep straight on, and then turn right at the next crossroads on to a narrow, made up road. At a junction opposite an ancient calvary surrounded with trees — with a view point — take the tarred road on the left for Bournonville.

BOURNONVILLE
✗ �

4Km
1

Cross the little bridge over the Liane, and in another 100 metres head to the right in the direction of Crémarest. The GR follows the D254 road for about 1 kilometre, then goes off to the left at La Drouille and climbs up towards the Desvres State forest. At first the route follows a wide, straight, uneven drive heading south-east through the part of the forest known as Le Montpas. Before reaching the D253 road, leave this drive and take a service path on the right which leads to the D127 road near the forest lodge at La Haut Forêt.

Forest lodge at La Haute Forêt
Detour *20 mins*
DESVRES
⌂ ▲ ✗ � ⚱ 🚌

6Km
1:30

Museum; potteries; bustling market on Tuesday mornings, especially the cattle market. Go to the left along the D127 road.

The next section of the GR120 heads generally north-west through the Haute-Forêt. It follows several service rides, and then joins a made up forest road. Just on the way out of the forest it turns southwards, to the left, for 300 metres along a narrow track which is not very accessible, and joins a tarred road. Turn right as far as the D254E road. Turn southwards, to the left, on this local road which takes you back into the forest. Leave the road and head

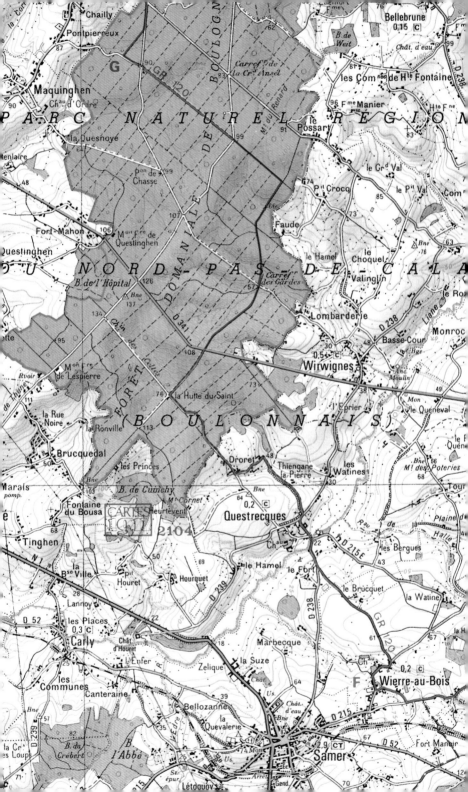

Intersection with the D341 road

5.5Km
1:25

LONGFOSSÉ
✗

2.5Km
0:40

Fork to the GR127A and the GR121

5Km
0:10

A little way beyond Sequières is a viewpoint at the top of the plateau shoulder, or 'cuesta'. This cuesta is a chalk formation, overlooking the whole of Boulonnais. It towers above Bas-Boulonnais with its hills of clay and marl. The cuesta is the shoulder of a chalky plateau known as Haut-Boulonnais, which is part of the Artois uplands. Chalk and flint are, moreover, used in the local

to the right along a service path — noting, on the right of the pathway, a large oak tree called the 'eight-armed oak' — until the path joins the D341 road.

As you leave the Basse-Forêt the GR120 follows a grassy track until it meets a made up road at Le Bouloy. Go left, to the south, along this road. At the Quatre Chemins crossroads keep straight on and take the Rue des Broussailles to Longfossé.

Before reaching the main square, turn right on to a minor road until you come to the junction with the GR121.

The link path takes a wet, sunken track off to the left. Cross the railway track by a little footbridge. You intersect another dirt path and turn on to it heading right. Cross the D52 road and head towards Longuerecque. Leave the tarmac path and take the first dirt track on the left. This then brings you to a made up road along which you turn left and climb towards the Bois de l'Eperche. Cross these woods and make for the plateau, where you follow a track at spot height 172 which joins the footpath GR127A, also called the Hills of Artois footpath. To reach the GR121, turn to the right along this cart track to Mont Corbeau, 174 metres high with a view point. A little farther on, level with a power line, you come to the GR121 close to the hamlet of Sequières.

Not far beyond the fork, the GR120 turns right and comes to Wierre-au-Bois.

*traditional architecture. The
flints are used in footings
and gables, and the chalk,
after cutting into sections, is
used to build the walls.*

WIERRE-AU-BOIS
♟ ▭

*Château; the writer Sainte-
Beuve, born at
Boulogne-sur-Mer, spent his
holidays in this village as a
boy; commemorative plaque
at the entrance to the
cemetery where his parents
are buried.*

Detour *25 mins*

3Km
0:45

SAMER
🏠 Å ✕ ♟ ⚓ ▭

*Museum; main square lined
with 18th century houses;
15th century church with
Roman font.
Follow the D215 road to the
village.*

From the mairie follow the D215 road to the
right. Cross a little bridge with metal rails,
leave the D215 and take a minor road on the
left. This passes a sports ground and then
joins the D238 road on to which you turn right.
This brings you to Questrecques.

QUESTRECQUES
Å ✕ ♟ ⚓

Old mill

1.5Km
0:20

Some 150 metres beyond the inn, cross the
river Liane and stay on the D238. At the
crossroads, head for Wirvignes. In another 50
metres the GR leaves the D238 road and goes
off to the left along a made up track. It crosses
a stream, turns left shortly beyond, and brings
you to Droret.

Droret

*The State forest consists
mainly of coppice beneath
groves of ash and
pedunculate oak. The ash
produced in Boulonnais is
much sought after, and is
used for example to make
tennis rackets and skis.*

9Km
1:15

Turn right. You soon come to the State forest of
Boulogne-sur-Mer.
At the Hutte-du-Saint crossroads turn right.
Cross first the D341 road and then the Gardes
crossroads. The GR keeps to a north to north-
easterly direction for about 1.5 kilometres, then
heads left along a straight drive to the north-
west. A little farther on the GR meets a forest
road and you keep straight on. Beyond a
hunting lodge, the footpath bears gently left
and then turns right towards the D254. Turn
left along this road to La Bellewatine.

La Bellewatine
Detour *10 mins*
LA CAPELLE-
LÈS-BOULOGNE

The GR skirts round to the right of a playing
field, crosses the N42 road and goes back into
the forest along the old track bed of a disused
local branch railway line. The GR comes to an

🏠 ✕ 🍷 🚉 🚌
Take a road on the left leading to the village.
Detour
BOULOGNE-SUR-MER
🏠 ⌂ ▲ ✕ 🍷 🚉
🚍 🚌

4.5Km
1:10
7 kilometres from La Capelle-lès-Boulogne. France's leading fishing port; beach; walled old town; Cathedral, Roman crypt, splendid dome; Column commemorating the Grande Armée some 5 kilometres away with view point.

PERNES-LÈS-BOULOGNE
🍷
Church dating from 1850.

Detour *15 mins*
PITTEFAUX
🍷
2Km
0:30
Château de Souverain Moulin.

Bancres

3Km
0:45

Maninghen-Henne
1.5Km
0:20

WACQUINGHEN
▲ ✕ 🍷 🚉 🚌

intersection and turns left — there is a pottery and craft shop worth seeing nearby. It then turns right as you draw level with a large stone flue and skirts a nursery of young trees belonging to the State forest. Turning left out of the forest, the path crosses the D234 road and heads west along a gravelly path. Just before a farm it bears right on to a grassy path and along the edge of a private wood. You are now crossing the valley of the Wimereux, one of the three main rivers in the Boulonnais region. Its source, like that of the other two, the Liane and the Slack, is at the foot of the cuesta. When you reach the next intersection, take a road to the right past Bellebonne farm, then cross a small plot of land to Pernes-lès-Boulogne.

Continue left along the D233 road and pass close by the church through the churchyard. Outside the church turn right and at the next crossroads climb straight on to the north.

Detour see left. At the crossroads, instead of going straight on turn left along the D233 road.

On reaching the plateau, turn right along the road heading for a clump of trees and skirt round it to the left. Just beyond the first house in a place called Hurlevent, turn left. The GR then brings you to Bancres.

Keep straight on at the crossroads, heading for Maninghen-Henne. Then at the next intersection keep straight on past a wayside cavalry which you keep on your right. Stay on this undulating road. You can see the sea from the highest point, where you turn left along a little service track for about 40 metres, then right, along a grass path heading southwest. This brings you to the D242E near the village of Maninghen-Henne.

The path follows the D242 road to the right, and at the crossroads you head for Wacquinghen.

The GR crosses the N1 road and takes a path that passes just to the right of the church. It crosses the railway bridge and then goes up a paved track, keeping to the right of the

Site de deux Caps

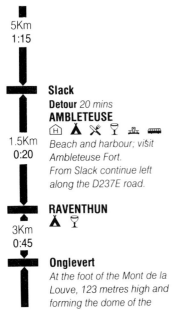

■
5Km
1:15

Slack
Detour *20 mins*
AMBLETEUSE
ⓗ ⛺ ✕ 🍷 🚉 🚌

1.5Km   *Beach and harbour; visit*
0:20   *Ambleteuse Fort.*
         From Slack continue left
         along the D237E road.

RAVENTHUN
⛺ 🍷

3Km
0:45

Onglevert
At the foot of the Mont de la
Louve, 123 metres high and
forming the dome of the

foundry. The GR takes the right-hand fork, staying on the gravelled track. It then crosses the D241 road, continuing straight ahead to the D237, along which it heads right and north to the hamlet of Slack.

From Slack the GR takes a made up track, called the 'communal' path, to the hamlet of Raventhun.

The GR crosses the D191E road and heads north along a local pathway which is made up at first. This brings you to Onglevert.

Gris-Nez Plateau; on clear days there is a fine view of the coastline from Boulogne to Cap Blanc-Nez and, in particular, of the cliffs on the English coast.

Detour *45 mins*
AUDRESSELLES
🏠 🏕 🍴 🍷 🚋 🚌
Typical fishing vilage. Follow the D191E road to the left.

Detour *20 mins*
AUDINGHEN
🏠 🏕 🍴 🍷 🚋 🚌
War museum; modern church of unusual design.

Detour *1 hr 15 mins*
CAP GRIS-NEZ
1.5Km
0:20
🏠 🍴 🍷 🚋

The closest point to England, which accounts for the position of the lighthouse, and why CROSSMA has set up a centre here. CROSSMA is the 'Centre Régional Opérationnel de Surveillance et de Sauvetage de la Manche' — Regional Centre for Channel Rescue and Surveillance Operations. The centre monitors the movements of 400 to 500 ships a day, not counting pleasure craft and fishing boats.
There is a marvellous view of the straits, the shipping lanes, among the busiest in the world, and England, when the weather is clear. Cap Gris-Nez marks the theoretical boundary between the Channel and the North Sea. There is a coastal footpath and a local, PR, footpath. Fact sheets on these footpaths are available

Detour see left. On leaving Onglevert, take the D191 north westwards to the left and then continue to the right along a track leading to the village.

Detour see left. Take the D191 road towards the village of Framzelle. Beyond the village turn left on to the road to the lighthouse.

*from the mairie at
Audinghen.*

The GR goes to the right of a farm and a transformer, then turns right on to a tarred road towards Warincthun.

Warincthun

At the crossroads 2 kilometres beyond this hamlet, the GR keeps heading north—north-east as far as the D249. It crosses the road and takes the second gravelled track on the left — the waymarking is unclear — then the first dirt track on the right. The GR cuts across the D238 road at an angle and goes on to skirt the Butte Carlin to the north. It then picks up the D238 road again to Wissant.

5Km
1:15

WISSANT

*During the Jurassic period,
150 million years ago, the
sea covered the area which
is now Cap Gris-Nez and
there deposited limestone,
sand and clay.
Later, some 100 million
years ago, the sea once
again invaded the land,
laying down the chalk which
appears as outcrops at Cap
Blanc-Nez.*

- Are you looking for accommodation in the Pas-de-Calais area?

  Our help is free of charge!

- Do you need to find a restaurant or hotel that will welcome a group of people?

  No need to worry, we will find it for you and make your booking.

- Whether you want a walking holiday, a sports holiday, a cultural holiday . . . .

  We will suggest suitable arrangements, whatever your budget.

- Do you just want a gîte for a weekend?

  We have exactly what you need.

LOISIRS ACCUEIL IN PAS DE CALAIS

Booking service

Comité Départemental de Tourisme
24 RUE DESILLE
62200 BOULOGNE SUR MER

Tel: (010 33) 21.83.32.59. or (010 33) 21.83.96.77.
Telex: 135543 F

ACCOMMODATION GUIDE

The many different kinds of accommodation in France are explained in the introduction. Here we include a selection of hotels and other addresses, which is by no means exhaustive—the hotels listed are usually in the one-star or two-star categories. We have given full postal addresses where available so bookings can be made.

There has been an explosive growth in bed and breakfast facilities (chambres d'hôte) in the past few years, and staying in these private homes can be especially interesting and rewarding. Local shops and the town hall (mairie) can usually direct you to one.

Agnetz
60600 Clermont
⌂ Chateau d'Agnetz
☎ 44.78.19.79

Amiens
⌂
Etang Saint Pierre
☎ 22.44.54.21

Arras
⌂ La belle étoile
Mr Théiot
☎ 21.58.59.00

Aubin Saint Waast
62140 Hesdin
⌂
Mr Vézilier
66 route de Lambus
☎ 21.86.80.48

Auchy les Hesdin
⌂ Le monastère
Mr Marecaux
☎ 21.04.83.54

Audincthun
⌂
Mr Bourgeois
☎ 21.39.52.17

Audinghen
62179 Wissant
⌂
Mr Delattre
☎ 21.32.97.48
⌂ La maison de la Houve
Mme Danel

☎ 21.83.29.95
⌂ Les Mauves
☎ 21.32.96.06

Audresselles
⌂ de la plage
☎ 21.32.95.12

Bavelincourt
80260 Villers Bocage
⌂
Mr Devogelaere
☎ 22.40.53.64

Beauchamps
⌂ Ferme de Lieu Dieu
Mme Maillard
☎ 22.30.92.23

Beaurainville
⌂ Le Val de Canche
2 grande rue
☎ 21.90.32.22

Belloy sur Mer
⌂ du Vimeu
☎ 22.30.20.58

Bernieulles
62630 Etaples
⌂
Mr Tillier
☎ 21.90.71.49

Blangy sur Ternoise
⌂
Mr Poyer
☎ 21.41.80.32

Bus les Artois
80560 Acheux en Amiénois
⌂ Le Château
Mr Déprez
☎ 22.76.26.83

Calais
62100 Calais
⌂ Le Georges V
36 rue royale
☎ 21.97.68.00

Campremy
60480 Froissy
⌂ ferme de Grand Mesnil
☎ 44.80.73.41

le cap Gris Nez
62179 Wissant
⌂ du Gris Nez
☎ 21.32.96.37
⌂ Bela Brise
☎ 21.32.64.84
⌂ Mr Calais
☎ 21.32.98.13

Chépy
⌂
Mme Leblond
☎ 22.26.21.61

Coulogne
⌂
Mr Geneau Marc
13 rue Claude Debussy
☎ 21.96.01.49
⌂
2 rue des Accacias
☎ 21.96.16.93

ACCOMMODATION GUIDE

Drancourt
80230 Saint Valéry sur Somme
⌂
☎ 22.27.51.45

Escalles
62179 Wissant
⌂ La grande maison
Mr Boutroy
☎ 21.85.27.75
⌂ Escale
☎ 21.85.25.09

Forest l'Abbaye
⌂
☎ 22.28.30.66

Frévent
⌂ d'Amiens
Mr Varga
7 rue de Doullens
☎ 21.03.65.43

Grand Mesnil
⌂
Mr Alain Vasselle
☎ 44.80.73.41

Guines
⌂
Mr Michaux
Rue du pont à vaches
la claire source
☎ 21.83.96.77

Hardelot
⌂ Villa Souleia
Mr Cécot
☎ 21.83.73.95
⌂ L'écusson
445 avenue Francois 1er
☎ 21.83.71.52
⌂ La Régina
185 avenue Francois 1er
☎ 21.83.81.88
⌂ Le picotin
☎ 21.83.71.28

Halinghem
62830 Samer
⌂
Mr Guilmaut
☎ 21.83.51.60

Hardinghen
⌂ Le p'tit bled
Mr Usal
☎ 21.85.01.64

Henneveux
62142 Colembert
⌂

Mr Leclerq
☎ 21.33.32.16

Hesdin
⌂ Les Flandres
Mr Persyn
22 rue d'Arras
☎ 21.86.80.21

Inxent
62170 Inxent
⌂ Relais Equestre
Mr Bourdon
☎ 21.90.70.34

Liévin
⌂ du Moulin
Mr Dupont
☎ 21.44.65.91

Loeuilly
80160 Conty
⌂ La Licorne
Mr Richoux
☎ 22.42.12.19

Longuerecques
62830 Samer
⌂
☎ 21.33.51.08
or 21.83.96.77

Longuevilles
62142 Colembert
⌂
Mr Dufour
☎ 21.33.30.42

Lonveaucourt Bailleval
60140 Liancourt
⌂
Mr Vidalain
☎ 44.73.13.93

Marconne les Hesdin
⌂ Les trois fontaines
Mr Ronger
16 rue d'Abbeville
☎ 21.86.81.65

Marquise
62250 Marquise
⌂
Mr Ellart Daniel
12 rue du Docteur Scheweitzer
☎ 21.92.98.49
⌂
Mr Lecoutre
☎ 21.83.96.77
⌂
Mr Vincent
☎ 21.92.89.28

Margny sur Martz
60490 ressons sur Martz
⌂
☎ 44.42.60.83

Menneville
62240 Dervres
⌂ Les Pierrettes
Mme Defieunes
☎ 21.91.65.54

Mers les Bains
⌂ SOPICEM
☎ 35.50.34.34

Montreuil
⌂ Bellevue
☎ 21.06.04.19
⌂ Château de Montreuil
☎ 21.81.53.04

Marlay les Ponthoile
⌂
Mr Bizet
☎ 22.27.07.11

Nédonchel
⌂
Jean Pierre Blanckaert
☎ 21.04.70.25

Orvillers Sorel
60490 Ressons sur Martz
⌂ Château de Sorel
Mme Richoux. Mme de Nanteuil
☎ 44.85.02.62

Précy sur Oise
⌂
Mme Gambier
☎ 44.27.74.16

Raincheval
80600 Doulens
⌂
Mme Lombard
☎ 22.76.42.67
⌂ de Moncourt
☎ 22.25.01.07

Saint Pol sur Ternoise
⌂ Le lion d'or
Mr Theret
74 rue d'Hesdin
☎ 21.03.10.44

Saveuse
80730 Dreuil les Amiens
⌂ Le domaine du cheval
Mr Lenne
☎ 22.43.48.24

186

Verlincthun
62830 Samer
⌂
☎ 21.33.54.44

Villers sous Ailly
⌂
Mr Fuzelier
☎ 22.28.02.11
⌂ STP
☎ 22.28.10.90

Wadenthun
62250 Saint Inglevert
⌂
Mr Butez
☎ 21.92.86.92

Wamin
⌂
Mr Lefèbre de Gouy
☎ 21.04.81.49

Warincthun
62179 Audinghen
⌂
☎ 21.32.97.77

Wierre Effroy
62720 Rinxent
⌂ du vert
☎ 21.92.82.10
⌂ La raterie
Jerome Coquerelle

☎ 21.92.80.90

Wissant
⌂ Le Vivier
Place de l'église
☎ 21.35.93.61
⌂ Bellevue
Avenue Paul Crampel
Mr Noujaret
☎ 21.35.91.07
⌂ de la Plage
☎ 21.35.91.87
⌂ Normandy
Place de Verdun
☎ 21.35.90.11

INDEX

Details of bus/train connections have been provided wherever it was possible. We suggest you refer also to the map inside the front cover.

Abbeville 103
Ablain-Saint-Nazaire 117, 161
Ailly-le-Haut-Clocher 103
Ailly-sur-Noye 29, 89
🅱
Ailly-sur-Somme 95
Aix-en-Issart 55
Ambleteuse 182
Amettes 128
Amiens 33, 95
Anaves 161
🚌 Lens
Ansacq 21
Antigneul (Farm/Château) 153
Anvil 69
🚌 Arras-Boulogne
🚌 Courtin coaches, Hesdin-Béthune
Arras 113
Assonval 135
Aubigny 35
Aubin-Saint-Waast 51, 113
Auchy-les-Hesdin 73
Audincthun 145
Audinghen 183
Audresselles 183
Aumerval 128
Avesnes 137

Bacouël 27
Bancres 181
Bavelincourt 39
Beaurainville 113
Beauvoir 27
Bellefontaine 133
Bellewatine (La) 179
Belloy-sur-Somme 99
Belval hamlet and monastery 155
Bergneulle 149
Bernieulles 59
Berny-sur-Noye 29
Beussent 59
Bezinghem 142
Bimont 139
Blanc-Nez (Cap) 165, 167
Blangy-sur-Ternoise 73

Bléquin 149
Blingel 73
Bois de la Ville 33
Bois L'Abbé 27, 159
Bomy 130
Bon-Secours (Chapelle Notre-Dame-de) 45
Boubers-sur-Canche 47
Boulogne-la-Grasse 83
Boulogne-sur-Mer 64, 181
Bouronville 175
Bours 125, 153
🚌 Saint-Pol to Béthune (4 trains in each direction, weekdays only)
Bout-de-la-Ville 147
Bouvigny Television Relay Tower 119
Bouvigny-Boyeffles 119
Boves 33
Braches 87
Bray 114
Breteuil 27
Bréxent-Enocq 59
Brunembert 152
Bucamps 25
Bulles 23
Busses-Bussuel 103

Calais 169
Calotterie (La) 59
Campagne-les-Guînes (Forest Lodge) 171
Canchy 105
Canchy (Maison Forestière de) 107
Capelle-lès-Boulogne (La) 179
Carency 115
🚌 Lens-Frévent
Carlepont 77
Caumont 141
Cavron-Saint-Martin 51
Chaussay-Epagny 29
Chaussée-Tirancourt (La) 99
Chiry-Ourscamps 79
Cires-lès-Mello 19
Cloquant 147

Cocquerel 101
Comte (La) 123
🚌 Lille to Saint-Pol
Conchy-les-Pots 83
Coquelles 169
Corbie 35
🅱
Cottenchy 33
Couple (Mont de) 165
Crécy-en-Ponthieu 109
🅱
Crécy State Forest 107
Cuhem 130
Cul de Sac (Le) 171

Dalles 143
Davenscourt 87
Dennebroeucq 133
🚌 Fruges-Aire
Desvres 175
Diéval 125
🚌 Saint-Pol to Lille, Berck-Lille
Dompierre-sur-Authie 110
Doudeauville 143
Doullens 43
🅱 Office de Tourisme, Rue Bourg
☎ 22.77.00.07
Drionville 149
Droret 179
Dury 91

Ecoivres 65, 114
🚌 Arras-Boulogne (5 trains in each direction on weekdays, 3 on Sundays)
Ecouflant 131
Ecouvillon (L') 81
Elincourt-Sainte-Marguerite 81
Enguins-sur-Baillons 140
Epainchen 67
Equihen-Plage 64
🚌 Caron bus company, Boulogne-sur-Mer
Erin 73
Escalles 165
Escoeuilles 152

**Boulogne to Saint-Omer
Estrées-sur-Noye** 29, 89
Etoile (L') 99

Faloise (La) 29
Fasque 135
Fauquembergues 145
Hesdin to Saint-Omer, Saint-Pol to Calais
Fay-sous-Bois 21
Febvin-Palfart 129
Ferté (La) 127
Saint-Pol to Bethune (6 trains in each direction weekdays, 2 on Sundays)
Fléchin 129
Flers 65
Folleville 29
Fontaine-les-Hermans 129
Forest-l'Abbaye 107
Framecourt 65
Francières 101
Fréchencourt 39
Fresnicourt dolmen 121
Frévent 45
l'Express coaches for Amiens and Saint-Pol, l'Oiseau Bleu coaches for Abbeville and Saint-Pol
Froidmont (Maison Forestière de) 23

Gard (Abbaye du) 97
Gauchin-le-Gal 121
Arras-Bruay
Gentelles 35
Givenchy-en-Gohelle 160
Golfers-Hôtel 61
Grand Mesnil 27
Grigny 51, 75
Gris-Nez (Cap) 183
Guerbigny 85
Guisnes 171
Calais

Halloy 43

Hamel et Pierrepont 87
Hames-Boucres 170
Hametz 47
Hardelot-Plage 64
Haut-Pichot 61
Haute-Escalles 165
Haute Forêt (La) Forest Lodge 175
Herain-Coupigny 119
Lens, Béthune and Bruay
Herbinghen 173
Hérissart 39
Herly 137
Hermelinghen 171
Hermes 21

Hermes (Le Mont de) 21
Hermin 123
Hernicourt 69
Courtin coaches, Hesdin-Béthune
Hesdin 51, 113
Arras-Boulogne
Dumont coaches, Montreuil and Saint-Pol
Hesdin (Forêt domaniale d') 51
Houdain 123
Arras-Bruay and Lille to Saint-Pol
Huclier 155
Hucqueliers 139

Jumel 29, 89

Lahoussoye 39
Ledinghem 149
Leulingue 169
Licques 173
Liévin 160
Lens
Ligny-sur-Canche 47
Litz 23
Loeully 91
Loison-sur-Créquoise 55
Long 101
⧫
Longfossé 177
Longpré-les-Corps-Saints 101
Lorette (Notre-Dame-de) National Cemetery 117
Louez-les-Duisans 113
Lucheux 43

Mailly-Raineval 87
Maninghem 138
Maninghem-Henne 181
Marbre et de la Géologie (Maison du) 169
Mareuil-la-Motte 81
Maroeuil 114
Arras-Boulogne (7 trains in each direction on weekdays, 3 on Sundays)
Marqueffles 119
Matringhem 131
Fruges to Aire-sur-la-Lys
Mérard 19
Merck-Saint-Liévin 147
Saint-Pol to Calais
Mesnil-Saint-Firmin (Le) 27
Mesnil-sur-Bulles (Le) 25
Mirvaux 39
Molliens-au-Bois 39
Monchel-sur-Canche 47
Monchy-Cayeux 69
Courtin coaches, Hesdin-Béthune

Mont-Saint-Eloi Abbey 115
Arras-Bruay
Montreuil 55
Arras-Boulogne
Dumont coaches
Montreuil-sur-Brêche 25
Moulin Blanc 155
Moulin d'Oecuphen 140
Mouriez 113

Nabringhen 173
Nédon 128
Nédonchel 129
Neuville (La) 35, 61
at Neufchâtel, 2 kilometres away, Amiens-Calais
Dumont coaches, Etaples-Boulogne
Neuville-en-Hez (La) 23
Neuville-Sire-Bernard 87
Neuville-sur-Ressons (La) 81
Nielles-les-Blequin 149
Noires Mottes 167
Noyers-Saint-Martin 27

Ocoche 67
Olhain 121
Olhain Departmental Leisure Centre 121
Darlin, Bruay, Béthune (Sundays)
Onglevert 182
Onvillers 83
Orval 81
Orvillers-Sorel 81
Ourscamps (Abbaye d') 77
Ourscamps Railway Station 77

Paraclet (Le) 33
Pernes-en-Artois 127
Lille to Saint-Pol
Pernes-lès-Boulogne 181
Petit-Houvin 65
Petit-Parenty 140
Petit-Saint-Leu 51
Peuplingues 169
Picquigny 95
Pippemont 129
Pittefaux 181
Pommera 43
Pont de Metz 95
Pont Terratu 140
Preures 139

Quesques 152
Questrecques 179
Quilen 138

Raincheval 39
Raventhun 182
Rebreuve-sous-les-Monts 123

🚌 *Arras-Bruay*
Rebreuve-sur-Canche 45
Rebreuviette 43, 45
Remaugies 85
Reuil-sur-Brêche 25
Rippemont 149
Rocquencourt 29
Rollancourt 73
Rosemont 155
Rumilly 137

Sachin-les-Pernes 127
Sains 65
Saint-André-Farivilliers 27
Saint-Aubin 135
Saint-Denoeux 55
Saint-Michel-sur-Ternoise 69
Saint-Ouen 99
Saint-Pol-sur-Ternoise 157
🚌 *Arras-Boulogne, Béthune and Lille*
🚌 *Dumont coaches to Hesdin, Courtin coaches Hesdin-Béthune, l'Express coaches Saint-Pol to Frévent*

Saint-Quentin-en-Ternois 47
Saint-Riquier 103
Saint-Sauflieu 91
Sainte-Bertille Spring 113
Salouël 91
Samer 143, 179
🚌 *Boulogne-Desvres*
Sangatte 167
Sanghen 173
Sauvillers-Mongival 87
Saveuse 95
Slack 182
Sombre 165
Souchez 159, 161
🚌 *Liévin and Lens*
Souich (Le) 43

Tachincourt 67
Thélu (Château) 170
Thièvres 43
Thubeauville 61
Thury-sous-Clermont 21
Tilly-Capelle 73
Troisvaux chapel 155

Val (Le) 147
Val d'Enquin 139
Valhuon 153
Valloires (Abbaye de) 110
Vauchelles-lès-Authie 39
Vaudringhem 149
Ventu d'Alembon (Le) 171
Verchocq 137
Verdrel 119
Verval (Le) 151
Vieil-Hesdin 51
Villers-sous-Ailly 101
Vimy Canadian Memorial 160
Vincly 131

Wacheux 128
Wacquingen 181
Wadicourt 109
Wail 47
Wandonne 135
🚌 *Fruges-Aires*
Warincthun 185
Wierre-au-Bois 179
Wismes 147
Wissant 165, 185
🚌